CORE FOUR
The Heart and Soul
of the Yankees Dynasty

Phil Pepe

TRIUMPH
B O O K S

The Library of Congress has catalogued the earlier edition as follows:
    Pepe, Phil.
    Core four : the heart and soul of the Yankees dynasty / Phil Pepe.
        pages cm
    ISBN 978-1-60078-811-6
    1. New York Yankees (Baseball team)—History. 2. Baseball players—New York (State)—History. I. Title.
    GV875.N4P525 2013
    796.357'64097471—dc23
                                                            2012051207

This book is available in quantity at special discounts for your group or organization. For further information, contact:

   Triumph Books LLC
   814 North Franklin Street
   Chicago, Illinois 60610
   (312) 337–0747
   www.triumphbooks.com

Printed in U.S.A.

ISBN: 978-1-60078-962-5

Design by Amy Carter

Photos courtesy of Getty Images except where otherwise noted

CONTENTS

FOREWORD

ON JULY 28, 1995, I WENT FROM THE TORONTO BLUE JAYS TO THE New York Yankees in a trade that, at the time, hardly set the baseball world on its ear. I was 32 years old—what baseball people like to call the "twilight" of my career.

I could look back on some very good days with the New York Mets, the Kansas City Royals, and the Blue Jays: 120 wins with only 76 losses, a 20-win season, and a Cy Young Award with the Royals, my hometown team.

With the Yankees, I was expected to provide a so-called veteran presence on a team of up-and-coming young stars. At the same time I would benefit by holding off the eventual limbo of retirement and the feeling of emptiness at the loss of professional camaraderie and competition. My reward would include another hefty contract...or two...or three, and the opportunity to feed my hunger for the kind of culture found only in New York: theater, museums, restaurants, etc.

People said it was a nice way for me to wind down a somewhat checkered career.

It turned out to be the best thing that ever happened to me professionally.

I got to extend my career by six seasons, win another 64 games, make three All-Star teams, pitch a perfect game, play for four World Series champions, and sow the seed that was to be my current career: analyst on Yankees games for the YES Network.

And I got to play with the Yankees' Core Four of Mariano Rivera, Andy Pettitte, Derek Jeter, and Jorge Posada.

When I got to the Yankees, it was only a "Core Two," if you can call a guy with a 12–9 record (Pettitte) and a guy with a 5.51 earned-run average (Rivera) any kind of "Core."

Before the season ended, the entire "Core Four" would be intact. Jeter—who had been up for a brief trial before I got there and then went back to the minor leagues—was brought up from the minor leagues again in September, never to return. Posada also arrived in September, though he only appeared in one game. The Core Four was here to stay, and it's more than just coincidence that starting with 1996 the Yankees would win six pennants and four World Series over the next eight seasons.

I am honored and privileged to have been part of those four World Series–championship teams, and to have been a teammate of a Core Four that consists of two certain Hall of Famers (Rivera and Jeter) and two others (Pettitte and Posada) with strong Hall of Fame credentials.

But I would be less than honest if I said I knew Rivera would become the greatest closer in baseball history, that Jeter would get more than 3,000 hits, that Pettitte would win more postseason games than any pitcher in history, that Posada would hit more home runs as a catcher than Hall of Famers Gabby Hartnett and Bill Dickey, or that this Core would stay together for 16 years and that three of them, all save Posada, would still be performing at a high level going into the 2013 season.

—David Cone

INTRODUCTION

Outlined against a blue, gray October sky .the Four Horsemen
rode again. In dramatic lore they are known as famine,
pestilence, destruction, and death. These are only aliases.
Their real names are Rivera, Pettitte, Posada, and Jeter.

—With apologies to Grantland Rice

SEVEN DECADES AFTER COACH KNUTE ROCKNE'S BACKFIELD OF quarterback Harry Stuhldreher, left halfback Jim Crowley, right halfback Don Miller, and fullback Elmer Layden were immortalized by Grantland Rice, probably the most famous of all sportswriters, for running rampant through and around the Army defense in Notre Dame's 13–7 victory before 55,000 spectators in New York's Polo Grounds on the afternoon of October 18, 1924, along came Mariano Rivera, Andy Pettitte, Jorge Posada, and Derek Jeter.

In time, they would come to be known as "The Core Four" and they would don the famed pinstripes of the New York Yankees.

And not a moment too soon!

Oh, how the mighty had fallen in the years preceding the arrival of these young saviors.

As January 1, 1990, dawned, ushering in a new year and a new decade, the erstwhile mighty, the exceedingly proud, always-arrogant, ever-pompous New York Yankees were in decline, a state bordered on the north by turmoil, on the south by dysfunction, on the east by upheaval, and on the west by instability.

They had not played in the World Series in eight years, and had not won one in 11, their longest drought in seven decades. They would extend that streak to 17 seasons without winning the World Series, their longest period of privation since the franchise's *first* 20 seasons in New York, almost a century before.

From 1982 to 1990, the manager's office was occupied by Bob Lemon, Gene Michael, Clyde King, Billy Martin (his third tour as Yankees' manager), Yogi Berra, Martin again, Lou Piniella, Martin once more, Piniella again, Dallas Green, and Bucky Dent. (Billy Martin was tragically killed at the age of 61 in an automobile crash outside his home in upstate Binghamton, New York, on Christmas Day, 1989. At the time there were reports that there were negotiations being held for a Billy VI as manager of the Yankees.)

While the Yankees' managerial carousel was spinning, the office of Yankees president/vice president for player personnel/general manager also was in need of a revolving door, as Lou Saban gave way to Gene McHale who departed for Clyde King who abdicated in favor of Woody Woodward who turned it over to Lou Piniella who passed it on to Bob Quinn who left to make room for Harding Peterson.

The turnover in managers and in front-office executives made the Yankees the laughing stock of baseball, which was reflected on the playing field. A proud franchise that could boast of Babe Ruth, Lou Gehrig, Joe DiMaggio, Lefty Gomez, Mickey Mantle, Whitey Ford, Yogi Berra, Reggie Jackson, Thurman Munson, Catfish Hunter, Graig Nettles, Ron Guidry, and Don Mattingly now was represented by such as Bobby Meacham, Joe Cowley, Steve Trout, Wayne Tolleson, Dan Pasqua, Eric Plunk, Don Slaught, Cecilio Guante, Clay Parker, and Alvaro Espinosa.

Alarmingly, attendance had fallen from an all-time franchise high of 2,633,701 in 1988 to a five-year low of 2,170,485 in 1989, and to rub salt in their wounds, the Yankees' staunchest rivals, the crosstown, upstart, formerly laughable expansion New York Mets had seemingly regained control of New York City, outdrawing the Yankees for the last six seasons by an aggregate of some 3 million paying customers more than the Yankees.

The Yankees restoration would begin on February 17, 1990, with a transaction that hardly made a ripple in the baseball waters: the signing of a slim, 20-year-old, non-drafted amateur, a free agent right-handed pitcher out of Panama named Mariano Rivera.

Four months later, in the 22nd round of the June amateur draft, the Yankees would select Andrew Eugene Pettitte, an 18-year-old left-handed pitcher from Deer Park (Texas) High School. Two rounds after choosing Pettitte, they would select Jorge Rafael de Posada Jr., a switch-hitting infielder from Santurce, Puerto Rico.

At the same time, a Yankee scout named Dick Groch was keeping a watchful eye on a skinny shortstop named Derek Sanderson Jeter, who was completing his sophomore year at Central High School in Kalamazoo, Michigan. The Yankees would make him their first pick in the 1992 June amateur draft and he would team with Rivera, Pettitte, and Posada to form what would come to be known as the Yankees' "Core Four."

The Core Four would play as Yankees teammates for 13 seasons, during which time they would make the playoffs 12 times, win the American League East title eight times, the American League pennant seven times, and the World Series five times.

In 2010, Rivera, Posada, and Jeter became the first three teammates in any of the four major North American sports (baseball, football, basketball, hockey) to play together on the same team for 16 consecutive seasons. (Pettitte missed joining the others when he left the Yankees to sign with the Houston Astros before returning to the Yankees and reuniting with the other members of the Core Four.)

It's a baseball anomaly that, more than 20 years after they were signed to professional contracts, all four—two certain, no-brainer, first-ballot Hall of Famers and two others who are borderline but in the discussion—remained active, important, and relevant members of the team that signed them. That might not be so remarkable a happenstance for one player, or even two.

But all four?

Considering the accepted short shelf life of the professional athlete and the perishability of athletic talent, especially among pitchers, this phenomenon can only be attributed to excellent scouting, rare clairvoyance, and, let's face it, good fortune.

1   ENTER MARIANO

MAJOR LEAGUE BASEBALL SCOUTS WERE NOT EXACTLY BEATING A
path to Panama in 1990, not like they were to San Pedro Macoris,
the Dominican Republic; Santurce, Puerto Rico; or Caracas,
Venezuela. In 1990, you journeyed to Panama to discover future
stars of World Cup soccer or for the shrimp and sardines, not for
baseball players.

On February 17, 1990, when the Yankees signed an undrafted,
free agent amateur named Mariano Rivera from the tiny fishing
village of Puerto Caimito, Panama, a transaction deemed so in-
consequential it never so much as made the agate of the New York
newspapers. Only 24 Panamanians had ever appeared in a major
league game, most of them up for little more than the proverbial
cup of Jaramillo Especial.

On the list of big leaguers from Panama were former Yankees
Hector Lopez and Roberto Kelly; catcher Manny Sanguillen, a
mainstay for the Pittsburgh Pirates that won six National League
East titles and two World Series in the 1970s; Rennie Stennett,
who tied a major league record on September 16, 1975, when he
banged out seven hits for the Pirates in a game against the Chicago
Cubs; and one Hall of Famer, Rod Carew, whose Panamanian

1

mother gave birth to him on a racially segregated train in the town of Gatun in the Panama Canal Zone. When Carew was 14, his family migrated to the Washington Heights section of Manhattan, where he attended George Washington High School, which also produced Manny Ramirez and Dr. Henry Kissinger.

Mariano Rivera was born on November 29, 1969, four months after Apollo 11 landed on the moon, 44 days after the New York Mets won their first World Series in a resounding upset of the heavily favored Baltimore Orioles, and eight days after the birth of Ken Griffey Jr., half a world away. As a child, young Mariano whiled away the idle hours playing baseball, but not with any thought of making it a career. Soccer was his game. Baseball was fun, a diversion played with baseballs handmade of fish netting and electrical tape, bats constructed from tree branches, and gloves formed out of milk cartons. When he was 12, Mariano's father bought him his first real glove. His formative years were good times, so good Mariano didn't realize he was poor.

"I didn't have much," he once said. "I didn't have anything. But what we had, I was happy. My childhood was wonderful."

Finished with Pedro Pablo Sanchez High School at 16, Mariano did what most Panamanian boys his age did: he went to work. Six days a week he toiled on a commercial fishing boat captained by his father. On the seventh day he played sports.

"On the boat, I liked looking at all the different fish," he said. "But my father's life was not for me. There's no future in fishing."

Perhaps he could escape as a professional soccer player. Baseball was not an option, but he continued to play for fun with Panama Oeste, a local amateur team.

If it was fate that brought a man named Herb Raybourn, director of Latin American operations for the New York Yankees, to Puerto Caimito, where he first saw Rivera, a 155-pound short-stop—"He had a good arm and good hands, but I didn't think he could be a major league shortstop so I passed on him."—it was good fortune that sent Raybourn back to Puerto Caimito to check out reports about a promising pitching prospect named Mariano Rivera. Raybourn was confused. The Mariano Rivera he knew in Puerto Caimito was a shortstop, and no prospect. Nonetheless, Raybourn returned to the tiny fishing village and arranged a workout for the young shortstop-turned-pitcher.

What Raybourn saw hardly blew the scout away, a pitcher topping out at 84 miles per hour, not the stuff of legend or future stardom. But Raybourn saw something special in the skinny right-hander: a joy for the game and a strong desire to excel. He also saw rare athleticism and an easy, fluid pitching motion that caused the baseball to jump out of his hand and enable him to get excellent movement on his pitches.

Raybourn reported his findings to the Yankees, who authorized him to offer the young pitcher a signing bonus of $3,000, tantamount to a king's ransom to a child of Puerto Caimito, Panama. Rivera eagerly accepted the offer, hoping this was his chance to avoid the life of a fisherman. It also was the only offer he received.

"I was there the year before and I passed on him," said Raybourn. "I went back a year later and we got him. Why didn't any of the other scouts sign him before I got back to Panama?"

Why, indeed!

Somewhat frightened and extremely naïve—he had never been out of Panama, had never been on an airplane, and he spoke no English—Mariano, considered nothing more than a fringe prospect, flew to Tampa to join the Yankees affiliate in the Gulf Coast Rookie League, the lowest rung on the team's minor league ladder. Rivera's Tampa Yankees teammates were future major leaguers Russ Springer, Ricky Ledee, Shane Spencer, and the Yankees' first-round draft pick that year, Carl Everett. Rivera's manager was 29-year-old Glenn Sherlock of Nahant, Massachusetts, a catcher who had been the 21st-round selection of the Houston Astros in the 1983 amateur draft and who had spent seven minor league seasons in the Astros' and Yankees' farm systems without ever reaching the major leagues.

Sherlock, now the bullpen coach for the Arizona Diamondbacks, remembers the young Rivera as "very quiet—he didn't speak a lot of English—a very nice kid that went about his business in a professional manner.

"Obviously we didn't know at that time that he was going to be maybe the greatest relief pitcher of all time. I don't know if anybody is that smart. What we did see was that he had a very good work ethic and he did a lot of the little things like the bunt defenses and the pitchers fielding practice. He put a lot of effort into it. He was an extremely good athlete.

"Hoyt Wilhelm [the Hall of Famer, one of the great knuckleball pitchers of all time and a pioneer relief pitcher for 21 seasons in the 1950s, '60s, and '70s] was our pitching coach and he used to play a game with the pitchers so they could have some fun. He'd let them bat and shag and Mariano could really hit and he could really play the outfield. He was clearly one of the best athletes we had on the team."

As his first season was winding down, Rivera had pitched in 21 games and had the lowest earned run average in the league, but he was five innings short of qualifying for the league ERA title, for which the Yankees offered a wristwatch and a bonus of $500.

"We had a doubleheader on the last day of the season," Sherlock recalled. "We spoke to Mitch Lukevics [director of minor league operations for the Yankees] and talked about starting Mariano in one of the games. We got an okay and Mariano pitched a seven inning no-hitter, which was pretty amazing."

While he still was not considered a hot prospect, the no-hitter, a 5–1 record, an ERA of 0.17, 17 hits allowed, and 58 strikeouts in 52 innings, could not be overlooked. At least it caught their attention in the Bronx and Tampa (where the Yankees' player development staff is located) and it elevated, at least slightly, Rivera's status. No longer merely a fringe prospect, Rivera was moved up to Class

A Greensboro in the South Atlantic League the following season.

At Greensboro, Rivera split his time almost equally between starting and relieving. Despite a record of 4–9, he continued to impress and progress with a 2.75 ERA, 123 strikeouts, and only 36 walks in 114⅔ innings. It caught the attention of Yankees manager Buck Showalter, who deemed Rivera's strikeout-to-walk ratio "impressive in any league."

Showalter was not alone in his judgment. The Yankees brain trust concurred, bouncing Rivera up to Fort Lauderdale in the high A Florida State League in 1992. The Yankees decided he was now a full-fledged starter. By midseason, Rivera had made 10 starts, had a record of 5–3, a 2.28 ERA, 42 strikeouts, and an especially impressive five walks in 59⅓ innings. Then he faced his first crisis.

Attempting one day to improve the movement on his slider by twisting his wrist, Mariano felt something snap. He had damaged the ulnar collateral ligament in his pitching elbow, requiring surgery and abruptly ending his season.

"People think he had Tommy John surgery, but he didn't," said Gene Michael, the Yankees' super-scout/adviser (as well as former player, manager, and general manager).

No less an authority than Dr. Frank Jobe, the legendary orthopedist who pioneered ligament replacement (or Tommy John) surgery, made the diagnosis and ruled out the procedure which would have sidelined Rivera for at least a year.

"The ligament was frayed and Dr. Jobe cleaned it up," said Michael.

As a result, Rivera's rehabilitation did not cause him to miss the 1993 season. However, the injury did present the Yankees with a dilemma. Rivera's rehab coincided with the MLB expansion draft required to fill the rosters of two new teams, the Colorado Rockies and Florida Marlins. While they still didn't consider him a top prospect—"He had a straight fastball, no cutter, and no movement," remembered Gene Michael. "He was mediocre at best."—the Yankees thought enough of Rivera to protect him on their 40-man roster. However, they failed to include him on their protected list for the expansion draft.

In hindsight, the Yankees' Mark Newman, who has been with the team since 1989 and is currently the senior vice president of baseball operations, remembered there were few back then who were on the Rivera bandwagon.

"When we signed Mariano in 1990," said Newman, "I don't remember anyone saying, 'This guy is going to be a major leaguer.' He was a very good athlete and he could throw it over the plate, but nobody wrote out the Mariano development plan that said he would someday throw 98 miles per hour, have the finest control on the face of the planet, would learn a cutter, and, oh by the way, that's all he's going to throw."

Either the Rockies or the Marlins could have taken him, a thought that sends shivers up the spine of Yankees front-office personnel and fans. But to their everlasting regret, both the Rockies and Marlins passed on Rivera and he resumed his career with a step back to the Gulf Coast Yankees and Greensboro.

At Tampa and Greensboro, Rivera appeared in 12 games, all starts, winning just one game and losing one, but posting earned run averages of 2.25 and 2.06 and holding batters to a .208 average. His star was beginning to rise in the Yankees galaxy.

2   HANDY ANDY

BEFORE THEY TABBED ANDY PETTITTE IN THE 22ND ROUND—THE 594TH player chosen in the 1990 MLB amateur draft—the Yankees selected Kirt Ojala from the University of Michigan in the fourth round, Tim Rumer from Duke University in the eighth round, and Keith Seiler from the University of Virginia in the 21st round. Each of them, like Pettitte, a left-handed pitcher.

Ever hear of them?

Among them, Ojala, Rumer, and Seiler would win 153 professional games—all but three in the minor leagues—almost 100 fewer than Pettitte's major league wins.

What this speaks to is the inexact science of free agent scouting in baseball. How else can one account for the fact that the same year the scouting department that was so clairvoyant in taking Pettitte in the 22nd round, Ricky Ledee in the 16th round, Kevin Jordan in the 20th round, Jorge Posada in the 24th round, and Shane Spencer in the 28th round could have been so much off the mark with Ojala, Rumer, and Seiler?

Clearly the Yankees and scout Joe Robison, who had been following Pettitte since Andy was in high school, were enamored with Pettitte's size, youth, and athleticism.

Born in Baton Rouge, Louisiana, Pettitte was nine when his family moved to Deer Park, Texas, a suburb of Houston, where his father, Tommy, worked at an oil refinery and devoted his free time to coaching his son in youth baseball leagues.

Not yet 18 years old as the 1990 MLB free agent draft was approaching, Pettitte stood 6'5" and weighed a somewhat pudgy, but athletic, 220 pounds. Not only did he pitch Deer Park High School to within one game of the state championship, he played center field when he wasn't pitching and was the starting nose-guard on the Deer Park football team.

The Yankees liked Pettitte's upside. But they had a problem. Pettitte's parents wanted Andy to go to college and there were several colleges putting the rush on him, including LSU and the University of Texas. There also was Wayne Graham, the baseball coach at Texas' San Jacinto Junior College, which was only a pickoff throw away from the Pettitte's Deer Park home.

An outfielder/third baseman, Graham played 11 seasons in the minor leagues and reached the majors for 10 games with the Philadelphia Phillies under Gene Mauch in 1963 and 20 games with the New York Mets under Casey Stengel in 1964. He became baseball coach at San Jacinto in 1981, and in 11 years built the Gators into the most dominant junior college baseball team in the nation, winning five NJCAA World Series championships in a six-year span from 1985 to 1990.

In 1992, Graham took over the baseball program at Rice University, which had recorded only seven winning seasons in 78 years up to that time. At Rice, Graham duplicated his San Jacinto transformation, turning the Owls into a national powerhouse that produced such big league standouts as Jose Cruz Jr. and Lance Berkman, as well as a College World Series title in 2003. Through 2012, Graham has won more than 1,400 games as a collegiate manager and has never had a losing season in 38 years as a high school and college coach.

Pettitte was 15 years old when Graham first set eyes on him.

"He came to my baseball camp and I taught him a pickoff move," remembered Graham, who had no idea that pickoff move would eventually confound and devastate American League base runners for years.

"When I was in pro ball [with the Chattanooga Lookouts in 1960 and '61] I was lucky to be with a career minor league left-handed pitcher named Bob Milo, who had the best move to first base in the minor leagues," said Graham. "I was amazed by him. I couldn't figure out how he was able to pick so many runners off first base, so I discussed it with him and he showed me how he did it and I taught that move to Andy and to every left-handed pitcher that came through my camps. Most of them didn't pick it up. Andy did. That's the difference in Andy. He listens. Of course he improved on it later on."

In his camp, Graham forged a connection with young Pettitte.

"I used to prepare individual written reports for every camper and I presented the report to them at the end of the camp," said Graham. "On Andy's report, among other things, I wrote that he was a good hitter."

Graham was able to follow Pettitte's progress at Deer Park High School and was eager to have him come to San Jacinto, but he was not very confident in being able to land him.

"We knew that this was a guy that could come in and win for us because he could throw strikes and he was left-handed and he could get the curveball over the plate," said Graham. "We hoped to get him, but we didn't think we could because Texas was after him. I don't know what we did right, but he decided to go to San Jac rather than go to Texas."

Whether the initial contact with Pettitte was a factor in getting him to attend San Jacinto is not known. What is known is that Graham played his trump card by telling Andy he reminded the coach of a left-handed version of another San Jacinto alumnus,

Roger Clemens, who happened to be Pettitte's boyhood idol. That did it.

"Ten years earlier, at San Jacinto, I had Clemens, who had this great work ethic. But Clemens came to me pudgy, which I mentioned to Andy, who also needed to trim down. I told him that Clemens had been able to correct that and I told Andy that for him to reach his potential, he was going to have to watch his weight. He was going to have to have a conditioning program. I told him I thought that was more critical to him reaching his potential than anything else because I thought his delivery was clean. I thought he was going to have enough fastball and he had great control.

"I've had better arms than Clemens and better arms than Pettitte but these two guys came in at age 18 with better control and better command than all of the pitchers I've ever had. And they worked hard. Another thing about Andy, when he was with me, he had this fire. I noticed early in the spring, he was coming in slamming his glove down and punching the dugout wall when he didn't do well. I thought he would break his hand if he didn't change. I told him, 'You're going to have to control that emotion if you're going to reach your potential. You can't let emotion control you—you've got to control it.' And I think Andy does that extremely well now."

The irony of Graham's discovery and his role in Pettitte's emotional transformation is that in 1999, after Pettitte had won 67 games for the Yankees and lost only 35 in four seasons, George Steinbrenner thought Pettitte lacked fire and almost traded him to the Philadelphia Phillies. Cooler heads prevailed and talked Steinbrenner out of what would have been an egregious error. (Coincidentally, 23 years earlier, Steinbrenner had to be talked out of trading another left-handed pitcher, thereby preventing Ron Guidry from leaving the Yankees.)

Had Pettitte matriculated at a four-year college instead of going to San Jacinto, the Yankees would have lost their rights to him upon his enrollment. However, by attending a junior college

Pettitte remained the property of the Yankees until the following year's draft, giving them 51 weeks to sign him or lose him. Consequently, the Yankees and Robison continued to monitor Pettitte's progress at San Jacinto, where he won eight out of 10 decisions and went on a diet of tuna and orange juice and a workout regimen that enabled him to lose 16 pounds, turn fat into muscle, and increase his velocity from the 85–87 mph range it was in high school to a steady diet of 91–93 mph fastballs.

As the 1991 draft—and the Yankees deadline—approached, Robison met with Andy and his father and offered the pitcher a signing bonus of $40,000, which was quickly turned down. Robison excused himself from the meeting and left to make a telephone call. When he returned, Robison upped the ante to what he claimed was a final offer, $55,000. Exasperated by the ongoing negotiations, young Pettitte blurted out, "If you give me $80,000 right now, I'll sign."

Without hesitating—or excusing himself to make another phone call—Robison said it was a deal. Pettitte signed with the Yankees just hours before the deadline that would have caused the Yankees to lose their rights to him.

"I should have asked for more money," Pettitte would lament years later.

Indeed, if he had refused to sign with the Yankees, Pettitte would have been eligible for the 1991 draft, where the Yankees might have redrafted him or he might have been taken by another team and signed for what scouts estimated would be a bonus in excess of $200,000.

Pettitte began his professional career with the Tampa Yankees in the Gulf Coast Rookie League where he made an impressive debut with a 4–1 record and an earned run average of 0.98 in six starts. In 36⅔ innings, he allowed only 16 hits, struck out 51 batters, and issued eight walks. That earned him a promotion to the Yankees' affiliate in the Class A short-season New York–Penn

League in Oneonta, a quiet, laconic town in upstate New York, practically in the shadow of Cooperstown, home of the National Baseball Hall of Fame and Museum. In Oneonta, Pettitte made six more starts and had a 2–2 record but a glittering 2.18 ERA. Also in Oneonta, he became a teammate for the first time with a future member of the Core Four, Jorge Posada, who, at the time, was morphing from a second baseman into a catcher.

Pettitte's breakout season came the next year when he was 10–4 in 27 starts, pitching for the Greensboro Hornets of the Class A South Atlantic League. His earned run average of 2.20 was second in the league and the best in the Yankee organization.

In Greensboro, Pettitte once again teamed with Jorge Posada, now a full-fledged catcher. Late in the season, up from the Tampa Yankees in the Gulf Coast Rookie League came an 18-year-old shortstop named Derek Jeter to join Pettitte and Posada, mainstays of the Greensboro Hornets and hardened professional baseball veterans of 20 years old, each two years older than Jeter. They put the skinny, 18-year-old boy-wonder future shortstop of the Yankees under their microscope, saw him commit nine errors in 11 games, and wondered what all the fuss was about.

Looking back many years later, Pettitte remembered his first impression of Jeter.

"I was like, 'Look at this guy. A first-round draft pick? Are you kidding me?'"

While their time together as teammates for the first time with Greensboro in 1992 was ever so brief, Pettitte, Posada, and Jeter still had not yet caught up with the fourth member of the eventual Core Four of the Yankees, Mariano Rivera.

After his success at Greensboro, Pettitte was moved up in 1993 to Prince William in the Class A Carolina League, where he won 11 games which earned him a promotion for one start to Albany-Colonie of the Class AA Eastern League. He pitched five innings, allowed two earned runs, and was the winning pitcher.

At that time, there was a raging internal debate behind closed doors in the Yankees personnel department over who was the better prospect with the higher upside, Pettitte or Sterling Hitchcock, a left-hander from Fayetteville, North Carolina. Hitchcock had been drafted a year before Pettitte and he had preceded Pettitte up the ladder with the Gulf Coast Yankees, Greensboro, Prince William, and Albany-Colonie, winning 34 games in four seasons and—much to Pettitte's dismay and envy—given brief trials with the Yankees in 1992 and 1993.

Gene Michael lined up in Pettitte's corner, saying, "I liked his determination and concentration just a little bit more." Michael was convinced that it was the competition with Hitchcock that brought out the best in Pettitte and motivated him to not only succeed and move ahead of Hitchcock but also to be a source of great pride for San Jacinto Junior College.

"Andy's a terrific person," said his old college coach, Wayne Graham, a sentiment shared by the current baseball coach at San Jacinto, Tom Arrington.

"He hosts an alumni golf tournament here every year to help raise funds for scholarships," said Arrington. "He's just a very genuine person. He'll come over to say hello and I'll bring some of my players over to the tournament and he'll talk with them about life and baseball and such. He's still a big part of San Jacinto College."

Pettitte hasn't forgotten his roots.

"I visited him in New York a few years ago," said Coach Graham. "He told me he still has the piece of paper that said he was a good hitter that I gave him when he was 15 years old and in my camp."

3   SOUTHERN EXPOSURE

THAT JORGE POSADA CAUGHT MORE GAMES AS A YANKEE THAN Hall of Famers Bill Dickey and Yogi Berra and hit more home runs than any Yankees catcher except Berra is not remarkable. It's not even noteworthy. It's a miracle.

Consider that Posada might never have had the chance to play professional baseball had his father, Jorge Sr., not fled his native Cuba for Puerto Rico to escape the Fidel Castro regime.

Consider that 645 players were selected before the Yankees took Posada in the 24th round of the 1990 MLB amateur draft.

Consider that Posada was drafted as an infielder and didn't become a full-time catcher until his second year of professional ball with the Greensboro Hornets in the Class A South Atlantic League in 1992.

And consider that Leon Wurth, the scout who recommended Posada to the Yankees, might not have seen him in a game at Volunteer State Community College in Gallatin, Tennessee, had Posada not left Puerto Rico to play college baseball at Calhoun Community College in Decatur, Alabama.

How does a kid get from Santurce, Puerto Rico, to Decatur, Alabama, "the River City," located just southwest of Huntsville and about 50 miles north of Birmingham; a city with a population of 53,929 in the 2000 census, of which only 5.64 percent, or less than 3,000, was Hispanic?

For the answer to that mystery, one must consult Fred Frickie, baseball coach from 1967 to 1995 at the largest two-year school in the state of Alabama, Calhoun Community College, named for John C. Calhoun, the seventh vice president of the United States. In his 28-year tenure, Frickie, who played three seasons as an out-fielder/first baseman in the farm systems of the Cleveland Indians and Boston Red Sox, won 669 games and six Alabama Junior/Community College Conference tournament titles. In 2009 he was elected to the National Junior College Athletic Association's Baseball Hall of Fame.

Asked how he got George Posada (at Calhoun he was never called "Hor-hay," he was "George"), Frickie relived the incident as if it were last year, not some two decades ago.

"My wife and I were going to Augusta, Georgia, to see one of my former players who was playing in the Pittsburgh organization," Frickie remembered. "I was looking for a shortstop, so on the way we stopped in Atlanta at Georgia Tech where they were having a high school all-star baseball game. Ellis Dungan was there. At the time he was a Toronto Blue Jays scout, but I had known Ellis because he was a coach for 25 years at Chipola Junior College in Marianna, Florida—a real great program—and every spring we used to make a trip down the Gulf Coast and I always played him.

"When I saw Ellis Dungan at Georgia Tech I said, 'Ellis, I'm looking for a shortstop. Do you know where one is?'

"He said 'No.'

"I figured he was just holding back and I realized sometimes you have to give something to get something. I had a boy's name in my book, a left-handed pitcher in the Alabama Junior College system that threw pretty good. I wrote the boy's name and phone number on a piece of paper and I handed it to Dungan. 'Ellis,' I said, 'this boy can throw about 90. You may not know about him.' Ellis took the boy's name and number. A little while later here comes Ellis. 'I do know where a shortstop is,' he said. 'Rio Piedras, Puerto Rico. You ever get one out of there?'

"I said, 'No, but you give me his name and phone number and I'm going to start calling.'

"That was George Posada. His daddy was scouting for the Atlanta Braves, covering Puerto Rico, and that's how Ellis knew about his son, who was looking for a place to play ball."

Baseball was in Posada's blood. His uncle, Leo Posada, an outfielder, batted .256, hit eight home runs, and drove in 58 runs in 155 games with the Kansas City Athletics for three seasons in the early 1960s and was their regular left fielder in 1961. Jorge's dad, Jorge Sr., had been a promising young player before fleeing his native Cuba, but he never got his chance in the United States. However, he worked as a scout for several major league teams, including the Atlanta Braves and Colorado Rockies.

As far back as he could remember, baseball was a part of Jorge Posada's life. He deified the late idol of Puerto Rico, Roberto Clemente, put him on a pedestal, but Clemente died in a plane crash in 1972, when Posada was a year old. Posada's first baseball hero was Thurman Munson, whose position behind home plate at Yankee Stadium Jorge would one day occupy.

A natural right-hander, Posada at a young age was taught by his father to bat left-handed. When Jorge was 13, his father decided it was time for his son to turn around and bat right-handed. It had been his plan all along to make Jorge a switch-hitter, just as Mickey Mantle's father had done with him a half-century earlier.

By the time he turned 17, Posada, who patterned his game after Tony Fernandez and Barry Larkin, had gained a reputation as an all-star shortstop at San Juan's Colegio Alejandrino High School, where he also lettered in basketball, volleyball, and track. He was on the radar of some Southeastern Conference schools and also of the New York Yankees, who chose Posada in the 43rd round of Major League Baseball's 1989 June amateur draft. (In that same draft they selected Andy Fox in the second round, J.T. Snow in the fifth round, and Sterling Hitchcock in the ninth round.)

His dad didn't think Jorge was ready for pro ball. He wanted him to get more experience—and no less important, to further his education—by going to college. Unfortunately, because his English was limited, Posada failed to score high enough on his college entrance exams to qualify for a four-year school. Enter Fred Frickie and Calhoun Community College. Sight unseen, and acting on Ellis Dungan's recommendation, Frickie made bringing Posada to Calhoun his top priority. He began a series of phone calls to Posada in which he laid out what Calhoun was able to provide.

"I could only give him books, tuition, and fees," Frickie said. "We also had some rooms for athletes on campus called 'the Cabanas' and they were available for $30 per quarter semester. All he would have to pay for was his room and his meals. Everything else would be taken care of. There was a girl in school named Mitzi Taylor whose mother was from Peru. Mitzi was bilingual, so I called her into my office and told her I was going to call Posada and asked her to speak to him in Spanish and make sure he understood everything I had to offer him. I made the call and Mitzi talked to him and Posada said he understood. A week later he called me and said, 'I'm coming to Alabama.'"

The Posadas, Jorge Senior and Junior, made the trip by automobile from Atlanta to Decatur, Senior driving, Junior, who had never been away from home, shedding tears much of the way.

"His daddy brought him in September and enrolled him," said coach Frickie, who climbed in his truck and drove to the gymnasium to serve as a welcoming committee of one to greet the Posadas.

"I remember standing with George and his daddy outside the gym and they were both crying because his daddy was going to have to leave him. George's daddy is a really great guy. He wasn't a stern father but he didn't put up with anything. He raised his son right. He wanted George to go to school someplace where he'd be forced to speak English. He might have been able to go to Miami Dade Junior College or the University of Miami. I don't know. But his daddy was wise enough to realize that if he went somewhere that had a Latino community, he'd be speaking Spanish and he'd never improve his English. I think another reason he came to Calhoun Community College was because all he had to pay for was his food and his transportation getting here. So we were very fortunate that all those factors worked out for us and we got a great player and a great person."

When his father left, Jorge climbed into the passenger seat of the truck and Coach Frickie drove him to the Cabanas which would be Posada's home for the next two years. In the back of the truck was a small refrigerator. Jorge got out of the truck and was walking away when Frickie said, "Hey, where are you going? Help me with this refrigerator. It's for you."

Frickie had picked up the refrigerator so that Posada would have more than just a bed, a desk, a sink, and a shower in his room and he'd be able to keep food in the room.

Lonely and homesick in a strange town, Posada felt disconnected and isolated. He knew nobody else on campus who spoke Spanish, was uncomfortable with English and unfamiliar with the culture. He had no friends and no peers, but he had Coach Frickie, who would act as his surrogate father. The coach drove his new recruit to practice and to church, occasionally took him home to dinner, and picked out his first year's classes. One of his choices was Spanish.

"I think coach wanted to give me at least one easy A," Posada said. "I spoke better Spanish than the teacher."

One time Posada was involved in an incident on campus that got him in trouble.

"It was nothing major," said Frickie. "No alcohol or drugs or anything like that."

The incident was not something that got the police involved, just some typical college student mischievous prank, but it was a violation of school rules and enough to force the athletic director to have Posada tossed out of the Cabanas. With nowhere to go and no money for an off-campus apartment, Posada was fortunate he had Coach Frickie looking out for him.

"Come on, George, load your stuff up in my truck," said Frickie.

Frickie took Posada home with him and put him up in a spare room with a bath and a bed he had furnished over the garage.

"I never called his daddy [about the incident] because it really was no big deal," said Frickie. "But I told Posada, 'When you go home for Thanksgiving or for Christmas I want you to tell your daddy what happened.' So he went home and he came back and I said, 'Did you tell your daddy?'

"He said, 'No, but I told my momma.'

"I love George Posada," said Frickie. "He's a great guy. And my wife loves him, too."

"We adored him," said Martha Frickie. "He was almost like family. He was so far away from home that he was unable to get home for holidays, so he spent a lot of time with us, especially in his first year when he was the only Puerto Rican student here. We'd sort of take care of him. We'd take him out to dinner on the weekends and he'd come to our house to watch TV.

"He was insecure with his English in the beginning, but by the time he left here, he was dreaming in English. I asked him one time, 'When did you start changing from Spanish to English?' And he said, 'About Christmastime, when I start dreaming in English, then I know I've made the transition.'"

That first year at Calhoun, Posada was befriended by a teammate named Steve Gongwer, an infielder from Jonesboro, Georgia.

"They became real good friends," said Frickie. "Steve was smart, a good leader, a good ballplayer, a really good guy and he probably was the reason George stayed at Calhoun Community College."

Gongwer unselfishly made Posada's comfort and getting his new teammate to adapt to campus life his personal responsibility. They lived next-door to one another at the Cabanas, played table tennis and pick-up basketball games with other Calhoun players and worked out together.

"I always felt like I was a good player who worked hard," said Gongwer. "Others might have more talent, but nobody would outwork me and then along came this guy with all this God-given talent and he worked three times as hard as I did."

So impressed with Posada was Gongwer that he called home and told his father that he decided to no longer focus as much on baseball and to concentrate harder on his degree. When his father asked why he came to such a decision, Gongwer replied, "Because I have met a major league player and now I know what one looks like."

Today Gongwer, who recognized that getting to the major leagues was a long shot, is a successful Birmingham businessman.

According to coach Frickie, "George hit great his first year with us, about .350, .360 with nine home runs. I had a sports information director tell me that of his first 36 hits, 21 of them were doubles (still the Calhoun record for most doubles in a season). I started out playing him at shortstop, but he made a few too many errors and I moved him to third and he did fine there.

"Posada's daddy had told me George could play shortstop, third base, or catch. I already had two catchers, a left-handed hitting catcher and a right-handed hitting catcher and both of them threw good. Just to see how George could throw, I put him back there one day and put a watch on him to see how he threw to second. He threw great.

"Two seconds flat from the moment the pitch hits the catcher's mitt until it gets into the hands of the second baseman or shortstop is considered a major league arm for a catcher. If you're over two seconds, no major league team is going to sign you as a catcher unless they believe they can improve you. When I put the watch on George I got him in 1.8 and 1.9. But I kept him at third because I didn't need him anywhere else. I have no doubt when the Yankees saw him throw that's when they decided to make him a catcher."

Posada didn't hit as well in his second year at Calhoun as he did in his first, but he still was good enough to make all-conference and get a scholarship offer from the University of Alabama while earning his associates degree from Calhoun.

One day, coach Frickie walked into the office of Calhoun athletic director Nancy Keenum and saw Posada sitting there.

"Keenum," said Frickie, "you need to get that boy's autograph before he leaves here. You're going to see him on TV someday."

In 2007, almost two decades after he graduated and had been on TV thousands of times, Posada returned to Calhoun for ceremonies honoring both Jorge and Coach Frickie. They were inducted into the Alabama Community College Conference Hall of Fame and the school retired Frickie's No. 33 and Posada's No. 6.

Posada was drafted twice by the Yankees. In 1989, they took him in the 43rd round, 1,116th in the nation, but the signing bonus they offered was low (about $22,000). Posada refused to sign. "I'm going back to Calhoun," he told the Yankees.

In the June 1990 free agent draft, the Yankees drafted Posada again. Fortunate that he was available so late, they selected him in the 24th round, No. 646 in the nation, between Mike Mimbs of Mercer University, Macon, Georgia, and Marc Tsitouris of Wingate University, Wingate, North Carolina. Knowing Posada had a scholarship from the University of Alabama in his hip pocket, the Yankees upped their offer to $30,000, and Posada accepted.

Jorge broke in as a second baseman with the Oneonta Yankees of the Class A New York–Penn League in 1991, batting .235 with four home runs and 33 RBI in 71 games. He led the league's second basemen in double plays with 42, but he also made 20 errors.

It was deemed by the Yankees that Posada's future as a second baseman was limited, but he demonstrated a quick and lethal bat, was a switch-hitter, and was strong and tough and possessed of the perfect build and demeanor for a catcher.

When the Yankees proposed the switch to catcher to him, Posada called his old college coach, Fred Frickie, who urged George to give it a try, that his road to the major leagues would be much quicker as a catcher than as an infielder.

Soon the transformation was afoot. Posada got into 11 games as a catcher for Oneonta in 1991 behind the No. 1 catcher, Tom Wilson, who was drafted in the round before Posada and who would play 214 major league games with the Blue Jays, Mets, Athletics, and Dodgers.

The Yankees sent Posada to the Instructional League in an attempt to further his development as a catcher. There he came under the charge of Glenn Sherlock, a former minor league catcher who had managed briefly in the Yankees' farm system, but in the fall of 1991 was one of the Yankees' minor league catching instructors.

"It was in the Instructional League that we started really working on a day-to-day basis with his catching," said Sherlock, currently the bullpen coach for the Arizona Diamondbacks. "I don't know who made the decision to convert Posada to a catcher, but the Yankees always had the best scouting and the best player development system in baseball and I think when they saw a player that had the skills that Jorge Posada had, they were always looking to find a position that somebody with his talent could fit and be successful at. To have that type of hitter behind the plate is such a bonus."

In 1992, playing for Greensboro, Posada was ready to complete the transition to a full-time catcher, playing just five games at third base. He caught 41 games behind Wilson, who got the bulk of the Hornets' work behind the plate, 89 games. (It was while he was at Greensboro that Posada became acquainted with Derek Jeter, who joined the Hornets for the final two weeks of that season. Posada and Jeter would become the closest of friends. In 1999, when Posada married Laura Mendez, an attorney from Puerto Rico, Jeter was the best man at the wedding.)

By 1993, his third year as a pro, Posada had shot past Wilson, who remained in Greensboro while Posada leaped to Prince William. His learning curve as a catcher continued, and despite leading the Carolina League with 38 passed balls the Yankees were impressed with his ability to call a game, his rapport with pitchers, and his bat. With the Prince William Cannons of the Carolina League he batted .259 with 27 doubles, 17 homers, and 61 runs batted in, which earned him a late-season call-up to Albany-Colonie of the Class AA Eastern League for 25 at-bats (seven hits, a .280 average), and the following year to Columbus, the Yankees' top farm team in the Class AAA International League.

He was still a few years away from Yankee Stadium, but Posada was on the fast track to New York, where ahead of him were 30-something Mike Stanley and backup Matt Nokes, who was never regarded as a good defensive catcher and whose offensive numbers were in rapid decline. High on the Yankees' list of priorities for the immediate future was the search for a younger, more productive catcher.

4 KALAMAZOO KID

BORN IN DETROIT, RAISED IN DETROIT, A DETROIT RESIDENT ALL HIS life, Hal Newhouser was the poster child for a hometown boy making good. He signed as an 18-year-old with the Tigers out of Detroit's Wilbur Wright High School in 1939 and a few months later, after appearing in 34 minor league games, made his major league debut with the Tigers on September 29, still some eight months short of his 19th birthday. He started against the Cleveland Indians in the second game of a doubleheader, allowed three runs and three hits, struck out four, was tagged with the loss, and never pitched another game in the minor leagues.

Five years later, Newhouser would begin a three-year run in the major leagues the likes of which has rarely been matched. From 1944 through 1946 he would win 80 games and lose only 27, pitch 20 shutouts, and strike out 674 batters in 918⅓ innings. Although this period dovetailed with World War II, when most of the best major league players had gone off to serve their country (Newhouser was classified 4-F and rejected for service because of a leaky heart valve; he attempted to enlist anyway, but was turned down several times), Newhouser was nonetheless acclaimed as the most dominant pitcher in the big leagues. In 1944 he was voted

American League Most Valuable Player (at the time there was not yet a Cy Young Award). He won the award again in 1945 when he captured the pitcher's triple crown of wins (25), earned-run average (1.81), and strikeouts (212). The following year he finished second to Ted Williams in the American League Most Valuable Player voting and remains to this day the only pitcher to win the MVP in consecutive seasons.

When he retired as an active player in 1955 with a record of 207–150, 33 shutouts, and 1,796 strikeouts (he was elected to the Hall of Fame in 1992), Newhouser stayed in the game as a talent scout, remaining home and covering the Detroit area with which he was familiar and where he was accorded legendary status. Now, in 1992, he was the enemy, covering the territory for the Houston Astros, who had the first pick in the draft and were paying particular attention to a skinny 17-year-old shortstop from Kalamazoo Central High School.

Derek Sanderson Jeter (he was not named for the National Hockey League star Derek Sanderson as has been frequently reported, rather he was named after his fraternal grandfather, Sanderson Charles Jeter) was born in Pequannock, New Jersey, on June 26, 1974, which links him with Abner Doubleday, who also was born on June 26, only 155 years earlier. Two baseball personalities: one, Doubleday, who is said to have invented baseball (apocryphal), the other, Jeter, who is renowned for perfecting it.

When Derek was four, his father, Charles, an alcohol and drug abuse counselor who had played baseball at Fisk University (like his son, he was a shortstop), moved his family to Kalamazoo in order to complete his masters degree from Western Michigan University. However, Derek and his sister, Sharlee, would return to New Jersey for a few weeks each summer to stay with their maternal grandparents, Dot and Bill Connors.

Derek's grandmother was a rabid Yankees fan and she and her young grandson watched Yankees games together on television and made occasional trips to Yankee Stadium, where Jeter relished in watching his favorite team, the Yankees of Willie Randolph, Don Mattingly, and Derek's baseball idol, Dave Winfield.

"When I grow up," young Derek told his nana, "I'm going to play shortstop for the New York Yankees."

Hal Newhouser had other ideas. He had been tracking Jeter since his junior year at Kalamazoo Central when Jeter batted .557 and hit seven home runs for coach Don Zomer. As a senior, a sprained ankle hampered him, but he still batted .508, averaged an RBI a game, and was a perfect 12-for-12 in steals, for which he was named 1992 High School Player of the Year by the American Baseball Coaches Association. Jeter also was a three-year letterman and an All-State honorable mention in basketball. A point guard on the Kalamazoo Central team, Jeter earned local hero status when, as a sophomore, he hit a three-point shot at the buzzer to beat rival Portage Central.

But it was in baseball that Jeter excelled. Newhouser was so impressed with his potential that he implored the Astros to select the youngster with the first pick, despite reports that Jeter was prepared to accept a scholarship to play baseball for former Detroit Tigers All-Star catcher Bill Freehan at the University of Michigan.

Meanwhile, the Yankees, with the sixth pick in the draft, also were closely monitoring Jeter at the urging of Dick Groch, their scout assigned to the Michigan-Ohio territory. It was going to be a hard sell for Groch. The Yankees in the George Steinbrenner era, always looking for immediate gratification, rarely selected high school players in the first round of the draft.

But Groch persisted. Although Jeter was a spindly 148 pounds— he was already past six feet tall and figured to get bigger and stronger—and had only 59 at-bats in his senior season playing in weather-challenged Michigan, Groch saw in the young shortstop a player with uncanny athletic skills and instincts, excellent makeup, and a tremendous upside. The veteran scout pushed hard for the Yankees to consider taking Jeter should he still be available when their turn came up.

"Jeter?" said Yankees scouting director Bill Livesey. "Isn't he going to the University of Michigan?"

"The only place he's going," said Groch, "is Cooperstown."

On draft day, June 1, when it was time to make a decision, the Astros, in a five-year slide since winning their last division title and desperate for immediate help, went against the recommendation of Hal Newhouser and opted instead for the winner of the Golden Spikes Award as the nation's most outstanding college baseball player, Phil Nevin of Cal State Fullerton, partly because they judged him closer to being major league ready than Jeter and partly because they feared Jeter was too rich for their blood. There were reports that with the University of Michigan scholarship his for the taking, Jeter would be looking for a signing bonus of $1 million, more than the Astros had budgeted for their first-round pick.

So irate and insulted by the Astros refusal to take his advice was Newhouser that he submitted his resignation in protest.

The Astros, however, would not be alone in bypassing Jeter. Picking second, the Cleveland Indians chose Paul Shuey, a right-handed pitcher from the University of North Carolina. With the third pick, the Montreal Expos opted for B.J. Wallace, a left-handed pitcher from Mississippi State. With the fourth pick, the Baltimore Orioles chose outfielder Jeffrey Hammonds from Stanford.

Next in line were the Cincinnati Reds, who were known to be high on Jeter. As the Reds deliberated, apparently vacillating between Jeter and a University of Central Florida outfielder named Chad Mottola, the Yankees contingent held its collective breath. When the official announcement came that the Reds had selected Mottola, a euphoric roar went up from the Yankees draft room, which had been set up in George Steinbrenner's Radisson Bay Harbor Hotel in Tampa.

On June 27, 1992, a day after his 18th birthday, the Yankees announced the signing of their No. 1 pick in the 1992 MLB amateur free agent draft, one Derek Sanderson Jeter, a shortstop from
Kalamazoo Central High School who received a signing bonus of
$800,000, some $200,000 less than he was believed to be seeking.
Ironically, the Astros gave Nevin a $700,000 signing bonus, so if
money was truly the issue, by refusing to go $100,000 over budget
for the No. 1 draft pick in the nation, the Astros missed out on a
future Hall of Famer who could have filled their shortstop position for two decades.

It's interesting to look back years later at that draft and assess
how it turned out. Others selected in the June 1992 draft, all after
Jeter, were Todd Helton, Jason Giambi, Johnny Damon, Shannon
Stewart, Preston Wilson, and Ron Villone.

Of the 48 players selected by the Yankees, only four others besides Jeter made it to the big leagues. Their second choice, No. 102
overall, right-handed pitcher Mike Buddie, had a 5–4 record in
five seasons with the Yankees and Brewers. Outfielder Matt Luke,
taken in the eighth round (214th overall), batted .242 with 15 homers and 40 RBI in 123 games with the Yankees, Dodgers, Indians,
and Angels. Left-handed pitcher Ryan Karp, drafted in the ninth
round (242nd), was 1–1 in 16 games with the Phillies. And right-
hander Mike DeJean, selected in the 24th round (662nd), pitched
for 10 big league seasons with a 30–33 record for the Rockies,
Brewers, Mets, Cardinals, and Orioles.

Of the five players chosen ahead of Jeter, Nevin played 12 years
with seven teams: the Padres, Tigers, Rangers, Twins, Cubs, Angels,
and Astros, while batting .270 with 1,131 hits, 208 home runs, and
743 runs batted in. Hammonds played 13 years with six teams—the
Orioles, Brewers, Giants, Reds, Rockies, and Nationals—had 824
hits, batted .272, hit 110 homers, and drove in 423 runs. Mottola
played five seasons with Blue Jays, Reds, Orioles, and Marlins,
batted .200 in 59 games, hit four homers, and had 12 RBI. Shuey

pitched for 11 seasons with the Indians, Dodgers, and Orioles, winning 45 games and losing 28. And Wallace pitched three years in
the minor leagues, won 15 games, lost 15, and never got to the big
leagues.

All five were out of baseball by 2008, while Jeter motored on,
piling up almost 2,200 more hits than Nevin and almost 2,500
more than Hammonds through the 2012 season.

To launch his professional career, the Yankees sent Jeter to play
for the Tampa Yankees in the Gulf Coast Rookie League, and
off went this teenage prodigy to conquer the baseball world. He
couldn't even conquer the Gulf Coast League. In his first game he
was hitless in seven at-bats with five strikeouts.

"When I went to rookie ball I made a bunch of errors," Jeter
would say almost 20 years later. "I couldn't get a hit for anything
and they tied this big, red Wiffle ball bat in my locker with a big
sign that said, 'Maybe you should try this one.' Now looking back
it was funny, but when you're 18 years old you want to go into
the bathroom and cry because you don't know who these guys are
and now they're making fun of you."

There was a good deal of crying on the almost-nightly telephone
calls to his folks back home as Jeter, frustrated, lonely, and homesick, experienced failure for the first (and last) time in his baseball
life. In 47 games for the Tampa Yankees he made 12 errors and batted a paltry .202. He was saved from total humiliation by a wise
and compassionate manager, Gary Denbo, who benched Jeter on
the final day of the season in order to spare him the ultimate indignity of a batting average below .200.

Despite his failure, the Yankees remained high on Jeter's potential and his future. They reasoned that his problems in Tampa
were the result of being away from home for the first time, missing his comfort zone, and competing against better players, most
of whom were several years older than he was. With the Gulf
Coast League season completed, the Yankees promoted Jeter to

Greensboro in the Class A South Atlantic League, where he could get more at-bats and, therefore, more experience and also become acclimated to the town that would be his home in the 1993 season.

At Greensboro in 1993 it all began to click in for Jeter and he started to display the potential that Dick Groch and the Yankees had seen in him. His offensive skills began to surface with a .295 average, five home runs, 71 RBI, and 18 stolen bases, but his defensive difficulties continued. By midseason he had committed more than 30 errors and he was visited by the Yankees' general manager, Gene Michael. A former shortstop himself who, at 6'2" and 183 pounds, was built similar to Jeter. Michael also had defensive problems in the minor leagues. In his first minor league season with the Grand Forks Chiefs in the Class C Northern League, Michael made 56 errors in 124 games. He impressed upon Jeter the importance of playing relaxed.

Although he made a staggering 56 errors in 126 games for the Greensboro Hornets, most of them on throws, he showed tremendous range in the field and an athleticism that enabled him to make some acrobatic plays. *Baseball America* named him the South Atlantic League's best defensive shortstop, most exciting player, best infield arm, and the 16th-best prospect in baseball.

Jeter began the 1994 season with the Tampa Bay Yankees of the Class A Florida State League, where his manager was former Yankees catcher and University of Mississippi football star Jake Gibbs, and where he batted .329 in 69 games. He was moved rapidly up the ladder to the Albany-Colonie Yankees of the Class AA Eastern League, where he batted .377 in 34 games before being moved to the Columbus Clippers of the Class AAA International League, where he batted .349 in 35 games. He had hit for a combined .344 average at three levels with 43 extra-base hits and 50 steals in 58 attempts, while cutting his errors from 56 in 126 games to 25 in 138 games. For this he was named Minor League Player of the Year by *Baseball America, The Sporting News, Baseball*

Weekly, and Topps, and was voted Most Valuable Player of the Florida State League.

Jeter might have played for a fourth team that year. The Yankees were contemplating bringing him up to the big club for a few games at the end of the season, but a strike cut short the major league season. Nevertheless, all of a sudden the circuitous journey that would take him from Pequannock, New Jersey, to the Bronx, by way of Kalamazoo, Michigan, appeared close to reaching its culmination for Derek Sanderson Jeter.

5 STICKTOITIVENESS

ON JULY 30, 1990, MAJOR LEAGUE BASEBALL COMMISSIONER FAY
Vincent came down heavy and permanently banned the Yankees'
volatile and controversial principal owner George M. Steinbrenner.
His crime was paying $40,000 to a small-time local gambler named
Howie Spira to dig up dirt on the team's star outfielder, Dave
Winfield, who had sued the Yankees for failing to contribute
$300,000 to his foundation, as was stipulated in Winfield's contract.

It was the second time Steinbrenner had been "permanently"
suspended from baseball. In 1974, after pleading guilty to making
illegal contributions to president Richard M. Nixon's reelection
campaign, Steinbrenner was suspended by then-commissioner
Bowie Kuhn for two years. Kuhn later reduced the suspension to
15 months and, in 1989, in one of the final acts of his presidency,
Ronald Reagan granted Steinbrenner a pardon.

The latest suspension by Vincent did not mean that Steinbrenner
had to relinquish ownership of the Yankees, but he was banned
from the day-to-day management of the team, which would prove
to be a blessing in disguise for the Yankees.

Steinbrenner's last act before his suspension took effect was to
fire his general manager, Harding "Pete" Peterson. A month later

Gene Michael, who had been working for the Yankees as a scout, replaced Peterson. It would be the second time he occupied the Yankees' general manager's chair. He filled it in 1980 and 1981, but was let go by Steinbrenner. This time, however, he would be able to do his job without interference from the meddlesome Steinbrenner.

Gene Michael was born in Kent, Ohio. He attended Kent State University, where he played baseball and basketball. He played a season with the Columbus Comets of the North American Basketball Association and was signed by the Pittsburgh Pirates in 1959. He played one season with the Pirates and was traded along with Bob Bailey to the Los Angeles Dodgers for Maury Wills. In November 1967, the Dodgers sold Michael to the Yankees. He took over as their shortstop and moved his family to New Jersey as he began what would be a long association with the Yankees.

Michael's playing career with the Yankees spanned from 1968 to 1974. He joined the team after they had dominated major league baseball with five straight pennants (1960–64) and left them just before they began a new streak with three straight pennants (1976–78). His seven-year tenure with New York was a period of mediocrity for the Yankees, who finished fifth in the American League twice, fourth three times, and second twice.

As a switch-hitter—or non-hitter, as the case may be—he batted a puny .233 in his seven seasons with the Yankees, hit 12 home runs, and drove in 204 runs. But he was a defensive wizard who specialized in pulling the hidden-ball trick. Five times in his career, Michael caught unsuspecting runners napping at second base. His modus operandi was a simple one. With a runner on second base he would first inform the second base umpire that he was up to something and to be alert. Once he had told the umpire what he was concocting, Michael casually walked over to second base and asked the runner to step off the base for a moment so that Michael could straighten the bag. When the unsuspecting, or naïve, runner complied, the baseball miraculously materialized in Michael's glove and the runner was tagged out.

Before long Michael, who picked up the nickname "Stick" because of his slim, 6'2", 180-pound frame, was a favorite of the writers covering the Yankees for his affability, his baseball wisdom, his storytelling, and his wit. (Referring to his hitting, he once said, "The bat really jumps off my ball.") He also put his Ohio upbringing behind him and became a popular and often-visible man-about-town in New York social circles.

When he retired, Michael began a relationship with the Yankees that, including his seven years as a player, has lasted almost a half-century, with two years out to manage the Chicago Cubs in 1986–87. In his time with the Yankees, he has served in just about every conceivable capacity, from minor league manager (Columbus Clippers), to major league coach, major league manager (two terms, 1981–82), general manager, and scout.

Throughout his years with the Yankees, Michael had an on-again, off-again, love-hate relationship with Boss Steinbrenner. They feuded, they made up, then they feuded again, and they made up again. While being a demanding boss, Steinbrenner nevertheless had deep affection for Michael and a great appreciation for his baseball knowledge and his eye for talent. Several times he refused to grant to teams in search of a manager (the Boston Red Sox, the New York Mets) the permission to talk to Michael and then rewarded Michael with a title, a promotion, and a raise in pay.

Meanwhile, for his part, Michael, while exasperated with Steinbrenner's meddling, impatience, and impetuous trading of players—especially young ones—admired the Boss' desire and determination to put a winning product on the field and was grateful to him for the years of employment and financial compensation.

With Steinbrenner out of the picture, Michael was able to implement his plan to rebuild the Yankees' brand. He held on to the team's young stars—most notably Bernie Williams—showed foresight, used his great eye for talent in pulling off brilliant trades (i.e., Roberto Kelly to the Cincinnati Reds for Paul O'Neill, and Russ Davis and Sterling Hitchcock to the Seattle Mariners for Jeff Nelson, Jim Mecir, and Tino Martinez), and built up the farm system.

PAUL O'NEILL

On November 3, 1992, the Yankees pulled off a trade of outfielders with the Cincinnati Reds, sending Roberto Kelly to Cincinnati in exchange for Paul O'Neill. It may or may not have been the best trade Gene Michael ever made, but it certainly was the best thing that happened to O'Neill's career.

In eight seasons with the Reds, O'Neill batted .259, hit 96 home runs, and drove home 411 runs. In nine seasons with the Yankees, aided by being in the midst of a more formidable lineup and playing half of his games in friendly Yankee Stadium, with its easily reachable right-field seats, O'Neill batted .303, hit 185 home runs, and drove home 858 runs. He was a four-time All-Star with the Yankees, played on four World Series–championship teams, batted .300 or better six times (including a league-leading .359 in 1994), hit 20 or more home runs six times, drove in 100 or more runs four times, and is among the Yankees' top 20 career batting leaders in home runs, batting average, doubles, and RBI.

O'Neill is the only player in baseball history to have been on the winning side for three perfect games (Tom Browning with the Reds, David Wells and David Cone with the Yankees).

Known for his fiery temper, O'Neill brought that competitiveness to the Yankees, earning the admiration of owner George Steinbrenner, who called O'Neill "a warrior." As a result of his emotional outbursts, when he retired, O'Neill left in his wake smashed water coolers and a legion of adoring and grateful fans.

Michael was a scout and a sounding board in personnel decisions when the Yankees signed Mariano Rivera, and he was the general manager when they drafted Andy Pettitte, Jorge Posada, and Derek Jeter.

Steinbrenner was reinstated in 1993. He returned somewhat more docile when it came to the operations of the team, but he still was the Boss. In October 1995, he fired Michael as general manager and replaced him with Bob Watson. But this time a more gentle, more submissive George Steinbrenner retained Michael, first as director of major league scouting, then as vice president of major league scouting, and finally as a vice president and adviser, all roles Michael much preferred to the heat that came with the position of general manager. And each time he got a new title, Michael also got a raise in pay.

After Michael left the general manager's office, the Yankees went on to win six American League pennants and four World Series with teams he constructed. His Yankees legacy was secure, not only as the mastermind of one of the greatest periods in the team's history, but as the "Godfather of the Core Four."

6   HELLO COLUMBUS

THE FUTURE CORE FOUR OF THE NEW YORK YANKEES GOT TOGETHER for the first time during the latter part of the 1994 season with the Columbus Clippers of the International League, but there was nothing to commemorate the occasion. There were no bleacher fans chanting their names at the start of a game, no recording of Metallica's "Enter Sandman" blaring through the public address system to signal Mariano Rivera's entrance into a game, and no postseason parade down Columbus' High Street in Capitol Square as the Clippers finished in third place, 6½ games behind the Richmond Braves in the International League West.

No credit (or blame) for the Clippers' mediocre season can be placed on the Core Four. The big names for the 1994 Clippers (and on the Yankees radar) were Russ Davis, Dave Silvestri, Royal Clayton, and Dave Eiland. Their closer was Joe Ausanio, who saved 13 games and would get into 41 games for the Yankees between 1994–95, with a 4–1 record and one save.

The manager of the 1994 Columbus Clippers was Carl "Stump" Merrill, a loyal and dependable baseball lifer who has spent almost a half-century in the game—most of his years with the Yankees—as a minor league player, minor league manager, minor league coach, major league manager, major league coach, scout, and general all-around troubleshooter. He managed the Yankees between Bucky Dent and Buck Showalter from 1990 to 1991.

The last year of Merrill's managerial contract with the Yankees was 1992, but he had been let go after the '91 season, so when the 1992 season started, he was at home in Maine getting paid for doing nothing…until George Steinbrenner called.

"He said he wanted me to go through the minor league system and he wanted every one of our minor league players evaluated," Merrill remembered. "That's when I got to see Rivera, Pettitte, Posada, and Jeter, all in the minor leagues. In Fort Lauderdale I saw Mariano Rivera pitch a game in something like an hour and 50 minutes."

That assignment completed, Merrill was then sent to manage the Columbus Clippers in 1993. A year later, his roster would include for the first time all four components of the Yankees' Core Four.

"All four were good players and considered prospects," Merrill said, "but to look at them at that time and project that any one of them would get to the place where they ended up would be a stretch to say the least."

Rivera started the 1994 season with the Tampa Yankees, moved up during the season to Albany-Colonie, and then to Columbus, where he would appear in six games, all starts, with a record of 4–2. In three stops that season, he would appear in 22 games, all of them starts, with a combined record of 10–2.

Andy Pettitte split the 1994 season between Albany-Colonie and Columbus, and his record at each place was practically a carbon copy of the other. At Albany-Colonie in 11 games he was 7–2 with a 2.71 ERA, 50 strikeouts, and 18 walks in 73 innings. At Columbus in 16 games he was 7–2 with a 2.98 ERA, 61 strikeouts, and 21 walks in 96⅔ innings.

By the end of the season, the debate among Yankees brass was which of their young starting pitchers had the best upside: Sterling Hitchcock, Mariano Rivera, or Andy Pettitte.

Merrill remembers the young Pettitte as "a stylish left-hander that could locate a little bit. I don't want to say that back then I thought of him as a top-of-the-rotation pitcher because in those days when I first saw him, he didn't throw very hard, maybe 88 to 90 miles per hour. I don't think anybody could look at him back then and project that he was going to be a No. 1 or a guy that would go out and have the success he's had, especially in the postseason."

Jorge Posada started and ended the season in Columbus, batting .240 with 11 homers and 48 RBI in 92 games, and he would miss almost half the season with a serious, career-threatening injury.

"The first time I saw Posada [in 1992] he was playing for Greensboro and he was the designated hitter," Merrill recalled. "When I asked about him, I was told that he was a second baseman but they were in the process of converting him to a catcher. And we all know how that ended up. Actually, Posada probably could have made it as a second baseman, but becoming a catcher was probably the best thing that happened to him. He ran well enough to play the infield and he had very good speed for a catcher until he got that ugly, ugly broken leg."

It happened on July 25, 1994, in Columbus in a game against the Norfolk Tides.

"I can still hear the bone snapping," said Merrill. "It was a play at the plate and if you had a picture of it, Posada was textbook in where he should have been. His foot was on the front corner of the plate pointing toward third, the exact way you teach it. Somehow, and I don't know how, the guy [Pat Howell] sliding into home plate got underneath Posada's foot. I don't know how it happened, but it happened and I can still hear it snapping."

Posada suffered a fractured left fibula and a dislocated left ankle. Not only was his season over, for a time his baseball future was in doubt. He made a complete recovery and saved his career, but he had a setback in his development as a catcher that would delay his advancement.

Derek Jeter moved rapidly through the Yankees' minor league system in 1994, batting .329 in 69 games at Tampa, .377 in 34 games at Albany-Colonie, and ending up with Stump Merrill in Columbus, where he sent a calling card to the Bronx by batting .349 in 35 games.

"What impressed me about Jeter right away was that as soon as he came to Columbus, he fit right in like he belonged," said Merrill. "He was not in awe of the situation and not taken aback one iota. And he played like he had been there all year. That was the first thing that struck me about him.

"The other thing that really impressed me about him is that he continually wanted to know what he had to do to improve. No matter how successful he was, he was still looking for ways to get better. 'What am I doing wrong? In what areas do I need to get better?' That type of thing, which is very rare for a young player, especially one who was having so much success. And it was obvious that he wasn't just trying to soft-soap the manager or kiss his ass to stay in the lineup. It was sincere that he wanted to learn how to play the game correctly and if he was doing something that was incorrect he wanted to make sure that he knew about it and he wanted to go out and try to do it right."

Derek Jeter did it right in Columbus; he's still doing it right.

When the 1995 season started, the Core Four was intact with the Columbus Clippers of the International League, but by season's end they would be gone to an even better place.

7 NEW YORK, NEW YORK

LET THE RECORD SHOW THAT ANDY PETTITTE WAS THE FIRST. THEN came Mariano Rivera, followed soon after by Derek Jeter, and, finally, Jorge Posada four months later. The "Core Four" of the New York Yankees each made his major league debut in the 1995 season within 127 days of each other.

After 42 wins and 572 innings in four minor league seasons, Pettitte believed he had a good chance to land the fifth spot in the Yankees' starting rotation. But he lost out to Sterling Hitchcock. However, because to start the season major league rosters were expanded from 25 players to 28 to compensate for the truncated spring training as a result of the player strike, Pettitte was kept on the big league roster as a relief pitcher. He made his major league debut on April 29 against the Royals in Kansas City in the third game of the season. With the Yankees leading 5–1, manager Buck Showalter summoned the rookie Pettitte into the game to start the bottom of the seventh in place of Melido Perez.

The first batter Pettitte faced was Wally Joyner, who flied out to center field. Pettitte then struck out pinch hitter Joe Vitiello looking, but Gary Gaetti singled to left. Gaetti then went to second on a wild pitch and scored on a double by Greg Gagne, who in turn came home on a single by pinch hitter Phil Hiatt. At that point, Pettitte's day was done. He was replaced by Bob Wickman. The Yankees would go on to win the game 10–3.

Pettitte pitched four more times, all in relief, without a decision, and on May 16 he was optioned back to Columbus. Changing places with Pettitte was another rookie pitcher, right-hander Mariano Rivera, who had won one and lost one in four games at Columbus, all starts.

Rivera made his major league debut on May 23 in a start against the Angels in Anaheim, a debut best forgotten and, perhaps, an indication that Mariano was destined to be a reliever. The Angels knocked him out in the fourth inning, charged with five runs and eight hits, including a three-run homer by Jim Edmonds.

Three more starts followed. On May 28, he pitched a solid 5⅓ innings at Oakland, allowed one run and seven hits and was the winner, 4–1. On June 6, at home against the Athletics, he pitched four innings, gave up seven runs and seven hits, and took the loss in an 8–6 defeat. On June 11, at home against Seattle, he was knocked out in the third inning, but the Yankees rallied to win 10–7. After the game, Rivera, nursing a sore right shoulder, was sent back to Columbus. Twenty-four days later came the eye-opener.

At the time, general manager Gene Michael was in negotiations with the Detroit Tigers for the acquisition of veteran left-hander David Wells. In discussing possible compensation for Wells, the Tigers had inquired about "that kid Rivera at Columbus."

Michael recalled seeing reports from Columbus that had Rivera's fastball clocked at 94 and 95 miles per hour. Michael was perplexed. The reading was some three and four miles per hour better than Rivera had previously recorded. Was this a mistake?

Doing his due diligence, Michael checked around with scouts from other teams. They confirmed the reports.

"Yeah," said one scout, "that's what our reports have."

"I thought so," said Michael who concluded that Rivera had finally built up his arm strength after his operation of a few years before.

"At that point there was no way I was trading him," Michael said.

Instead, he made plans to bring Rivera back from Columbus and instructed manager Buck Showalter to clear a date for Rivera to start. It came against the White Sox in Chicago on the Fourth of July, George M. Steinbrenner's 65th birthday. Mariano pitched eight innings, allowed no runs and two hits, and struck out 11 in a 4–1 victory that convinced even his most vocal detractors that the Yankees might have something special in the young Panamanian.

In his rookie season, Rivera would appear in 19 games, 10 of them starts, with mixed results. While he won five games and lost only three, he had a bloated earned run average of 5.51, allowed 11 home runs, walked 30 batters, and struck out only 51 in 67 innings—hardly the sort of numbers to conjure up images of greatness.

However, starting on August 1, the difference in his numbers between when he started a game and when he appeared in relief was stark. In two starts over 10 innings, he allowed 10 runs and 14 hits. In nine relief appearances, over 17 innings, he allowed eight runs and seven hits. And in his last six appearances covering six innings, he allowed three runs and two hits. A pattern had been established that soon would be familiar.

Pettitte returned from Columbus on May 27 to start against the Athletics in Oakland. He pitched 5⅓ innings and allowed seven hits and three runs, one earned. He was the losing pitcher (his first major league decision) in a 3–0 defeat. His first victory came on June 7 in Yankee Stadium, when Pettitte pitched seven innings in a 6–1 victory over the Oakland Athletics. Pettitte took his regular turn in the starting rotation and would make 26 consecutive starts, winning 12, pitching three complete games, and averaging almost seven innings a start.

Pettitte's 12–9 record and 4.17 ERA earned him a third-place finish in the American League Rookie of the Year voting behind Minnesota's Marty Cordova and California's Garret Anderson.

On May 29, Derek Jeter's name appeared in a major league box score for the first time. He had been brought up from Columbus to replace veteran shortstop Tony Fernandez, who was placed on the disabled list with a strained ribcage muscle. Starting at shortstop and batting ninth against the Mariners in the Kingdome, Jeter was hitless in five at-bats—a pop-fly to short right field, a ground ball to shortstop, a line drive to right, a ground ball to second base, and a strikeout—in the Yankees 8–7 defeat in a four-hour-and-five-minute, 12-inning game.

Jeter got his first major league hit the following day. Leading off the top of the fifth, he sliced a ground ball through the left side off Tim Belcher and scored his first run later in the inning on a double by Jim Leyritz. A day later, again in the top of the fifth, he bagged his first major league RBI when he singled home Danny Tartabull, and this time it came against a brand name, "the Big Unit," Randy Johnson, who would finish the season with a record of 18–2 and win his first of five Cy Young Awards, before ending his career with 303 wins, two no-hitters, and 4,875 strikeouts (second all-time to Nolan Ryan).

Jeter would start 13 consecutive games at shortstop, batting .234, with three doubles and six RBI before being sent back to Columbus on June 6. He would return to the Yankees in September and appear in two more games.

The last member of the Core Four, Jorge Posada, came to the Yankees as a September call-up in 1995 and managed to get into one game. On September 4 in Yankee Stadium, with the Yankees blowing out the Seattle Mariners 13–3, manager Buck Showalter made wholesale changes in the ninth inning. Russ Davis replaced Wade Boggs, Gerald Williams replaced Don Mattingly, and Derek Jeter came in and replaced Tony Fernandez at shortstop. Joe Ausanio, a right-handed pitcher from Kingston, New York, replaced Andy Pettitte on the mound. And Posada, making his major league debut, took over for Jim Leyritz behind the plate.

In announcing the changes, the stadium public address announcer introduced the new catcher as "Jorge Posado," a slip of the tongue that would not be lost on his teammates, especially the impish Jeter. From that day on, the Yankees catcher had a nickname. He was "Sado."

Greg Pirkl, the first batter to hit with Jorge Posada behind the plate in a major league game, popped to third. Chris Widger, the next batter, struck out for Posada's first major league putout. Felix Fermin singled and Alex Diaz grounded out, first baseman Dion James to Ausanio, and Jorge Posada was the catcher on a winning team in a major league game on his way to shake hands with the pitcher for the first of hundreds of times.

Posada, Rivera, and Pettitte all saw some action in the postseason. Among the Core Four, only Jeter would not participate in the Division Series in which the Yankees were eliminated in five games by the Seattle Mariners.

The Yankees had jumped out in the Division Series by winning Game 1 at home, a 9–6 slugfest. They then sent rookie Pettitte to the mound to start Game 2, which turned into a 15-inning marathon. Although he wasn't dominant, Pettitte managed to keep his team in the game, which would become a Pettitte trademark in the postseason. He left after seven innings with the score tied 4–4. John Wetteland, the Yankees' closer and their third pitcher in the game, entered with one out and a runner on second in the top of the ninth and pitched out of the jam by striking out Vince Coleman and Luis Sojo.

Used ostensibly as a one-inning man in the regular season, Wetteland was still on the mound in the top of the 12th when, after disposing of the first two batters, he was tagged for a home run by Ken Griffey Jr., putting the Mariners ahead 5–4. When Edgar Martinez followed with a single, Wetteland was replaced by the rookie Mariano Rivera, who promptly struck out Jay Buhner to end the inning.

Down to their final out, the Yankees tied the score in the bottom of the 12th on an RBI double by Ruben Sierra that scored pinch-runner Posada with the tying run, and the game played on. So did Mariano Rivera. He would pitch 3⅓ innings, allow only two hits, strike out five, and be credited with the win on Jim Leyritz's two-run home run in the bottom of the 15th.

It was a portent, by far the most important performance of Rivera's brief major league career to that point, and the first time he would show even a trace of the greatness that was to come over the next two decades. It also would become the center of criticism over Buck Showalter's use (or lack thereof) of Rivera in the play-offs, which many believe cost the manager his job.

8 "CLUELESS JOE"

THE 1996 SEASON WAS ONE OF TRANSITION FOR THE NEW YORK Yankees. George Steinbrenner was still the man in charge, however, after his reinstatement following his two-year suspension and nearing his 66th birthday, he seemed content to begin the process of winding down and letting "the elephants into the tent."

After five years as general manager, Gene Michael stepped down after the season to assume his preferred role as director of major league scouting. Bob Watson replaced Michael as general manager, ably assisted by young Brian Cashman, Michael's right-hand man. Cashman would assume the same role under Watson, but they both continued to rely on Michael's expertise in the area of player procurement to improve the team as he had done so skillfully in Steinbrenner's absence.

Before leaving the GM's office, Michael had begun the process of engineering several significant and vital deals in the off-season between the 1995 and 1996 seasons. With Don Mattingly in decline because of age and a chronic bad back, Michael identified his top priority as finding a replacement to take over first base for Mattingly. He settled on Tino Martinez of the Seattle Mariners. Looking to stock their roster with young talent, the Mariners were willing to part with Martinez and asked the Yankees for third baseman Russ Davis and a young pitcher, either Sterling Hitchcock or Andy Pettitte.

Long a supporter of Pettitte, Michael held his ground and succeeded in persuading the Mariners to take Hitchcock in the deal along with Davis in exchange for Martinez and relief pitchers Jeff Nelson and Jim Mecir.

TINO MARTINEZ

Another great trade engineered by Gene Michael was a five-player deal on December 7, 1995, that brought Tino Martinez to the Yankees from the Seattle Mariners to fill the first base position vacated by the retiring Don Mattingly, one of the most popular players in Yankees history. It made for a difficult introduction to New York when the Tampa-born Martinez got off to a slow start and was booed at Yankee Stadium.

Slowly, as Martinez grew acclimated to his new surroundings, he began to hit, and soon he was winning over the fans. He finished his first season in the Bronx with a .292 average, 25 home runs, and 117 RBI. The next year he batted .296 with 44 home runs and 141 RBI.

Martinez's Yankee years are marked by two clutch World Series home runs. In Game 1 of the 1998 Series against the San Diego Padres, his grand slam off Mark Langston in the seventh inning broke a 5–5 tie and the Yankees went on to win the game 9–6 on their way to sweeping the Series. In 2001, the Yankees were down to the Arizona Diamondbacks two games to one in the World Series and 3–1 in Game 4. With two outs in the bottom of the ninth, Martinez belted a game-tying home run off Byung-Hyun Kim to send the game into extra innings.

After the 2001 season, Martinez signed with the St. Louis Cardinals as a free agent; played a year with his hometown team, the Tampa Bay Rays; and came back for one last year with the Yankees. He retired after the 2005 season. When he was introduced at the Yankees' annual Old Timers Day in 2011, this man, who was once booed mightily by fans at Yankee Stadium, got one of the loudest and longest ovations.

Michael was also instrumental in deals that brought catcher Joe Girardi in a trade with the Colorado Rockies; outfielder Tim Raines, who came over in a trade with the Chicago White Sox; pitcher David Cone, plucked from the Toronto Blue Jays for three minor leaguers; as well as second baseman Mariano Duncan and pitchers Kenny Rogers and Dwight Gooden, all signed as free agents.

For the stretch run of 1996, the Yankees would pick up sluggers Cecil Fielder in a trade with the Detroit Tigers, and Darryl Strawberry, purchased from the St. Paul Saints of the independent Northern League. They would also reacquire third baseman Charlie Hayes in a trade with the Pittsburgh Pirates (they had obtained Hayes from the Phillies for the 1992 season, but lost him in November of that year to the Colorado Rockies in the expansion draft).

But the most prominent acquisition (it also would prove to be the most important) was in the manager's office, where young Buck Showalter had been for the previous four years. Given the reins at the age of 36 in 1992, Showalter improved the Yankees by five games and moved them up from fifth place in the American League East to fourth.

The improvement continued for the Yankees under Showalter over the next few years. He led the team to a second-place finish in 1993 with 88 wins, and in 1994 he was on his way to leading the Yankees to their first pennant in 13 years. On August 12, the Yankees had a record of 70–43 and a 6½ game lead over the Baltimore Orioles in the AL East when players walked off the job, touching off the longest and most damaging work stoppage in sports history. It caused the cancellation of more than 1,000 games, including the 1994 playoffs and World Series, and it would last 232 days and extend into the start of the 1995 season.

The Yankees slipped a notch in 1995, finishing second to the Boston Red Sox, but managed to obtain a playoff spot and engage the Seattle Mariners in the Division Series. The Yankees won the first two games of the best-of-five series at home, 9–6 in Game 1 with Wade Boggs and Bernie Williams each slamming out three hits and Boggs and Ruben Sierra hitting home runs, and 7–5 in Game 2 on Jim Leyritz's two-run home run in the bottom of the 15th and Mariano Rivera pitching 3⅓ innings of two-hit, shutout relief to get the win.

The Yankees then flew to Seattle, needing only one win in three games to advance to the American League Championship Series. But the Mariners were a sleeping giant getting ready to awaken and they did just that over the weekend of October 6, 7, and 8.

In Game 3, Tino Martinez burned his soon-to-be-new team and new teammates with three hits and three RBI in a 7–4 Seattle victory.

In Game 4, Edgar Martinez blasted two home runs and a single and drove in seven in the Mariners 11–8 shootout victory that tied the series and brought it down to the climactic fifth game.

Edgar Martinez struck again with three more hits in Game 5, the last of the three—and his 12th hit of the series—a double off Jack McDowell in the bottom of the 11th to drive in the winning run and send the Mariners to the ALCS and the Yankees on vacation.

George Steinbrenner was inconsolable in defeat, while criticism rained down on Showalter over his handling of the bullpen.

Why, after Mariano Rivera had pitched 4⅔ innings of shutout, two-hit, seven-strikeout ball in Games 2 and 3, did Showalter not bring him into Game 4 with the score tied? He sat in the bullpen while the Mariners scored five runs against John Wetteland and Steve Howe en route to an 11–8 victory.

Why, in the climactic fifth game after he had pitched a scoreless two-thirds of an inning, was Rivera removed with the score tied in the bottom of the ninth and replaced by Jack McDowell? The Yankees pushed across a run in the top of the 11th, but Martinez's two-run double was the deciding factor, leading the Mariners to a 6–5 victory and a trip to the ALCS.

Veteran baseball men and media critics concluded that it was a trust issue, and Showalter's unwillingness to trust Rivera in critical, high-pressure situations doomed the Yankees and, as it would turn out, also Showalter.

During the season, Steinbrenner's closest advisors, fearing Showalter might defect to another team, implored Steinbrenner to tie up his manager with a long-term contract. But the Boss refused to heed the advice. He was determined to replace his manager over the objections of both general manager Michael and Michael's assistant, Cashman.

In a gesture of compromise, Steinbrenner offered Showalter a new two-year contract calling for a salary in excess of $1 million, but with the condition that Showalter replace his hitting instructor, Rick Down. When Showalter declined, Steinbrenner took it as Buck's resignation and somewhat gratuitously issued a statement wishing "Buck and his fine little family nothing but the best."

Although Steinbrenner recognized the youthful enthusiasm and vitality Showalter brought to the job, as well as his feistiness and inventiveness, he also saw Showalter as a control freak. Steinbrenner presumably believed one control freak in the organization was enough, so he set the wheels in motion to find a new manager for the Yankees.

While continuing to maintain that Showalter was the best man for the job, Michael nonetheless conceded that Steinbrenner was adamant about wanting Showalter gone and he recommended Joe Torre, recently let go by the St. Louis Cardinals. When the recommendation was endorsed by Arthur Richman, a trusted Steinbrenner lieutenant who had known Torre when they both worked for the New York Mets, Steinbrenner offered the job to Torre, who readily accepted.

While Torre was a native New Yorker who was immensely popular with the media and fans, and in spite of having been an outstanding player who had a lifetime batting average of .297 with three teams over 18 seasons, as well as having won a batting title and a Most Valuable Player trophy in 1971, his record as a manager was less than distinguished. In 15 seasons with the Mets, Atlanta Braves, and St. Louis Cardinals, he had a record of 894–1,003, a winning percentage of .471, and had made the postseason just once, in 1982 when his Braves suffered a three-game sweep to the St. Louis Cardinals in the National League Championship Series.

Despite his popularity and his roots, the local media was not greeting the choice of Joe Torre as the new manager of the Yankees with enthusiastic support. The *New York Daily News*, in fact, in a blaring headline, referred to him as "Clueless Joe."

9   A SPECIAL ROOKIE

THE YANKEES TEAM THAT JOE TORRE TOOK OVER IN THE SPRING of 1996 was largely a veteran one with established major leaguers manning most positions—Wade Boggs at third base, Bernie Williams and Paul O'Neill in center field and right, switch-hitting Ruben Sierra the full-time designated hitter.

The pitching staff had talent, experience, and a resume of success. It included holdovers David Cone and Jimmy Key—proven big winners in the major leagues—and second-year left-hander Andy Pettitte. Jack McDowell had left to test free agency, but the Yankees had added left-hander Kenny Rogers and right-hander Dwight "Doc" Gooden as free agents of their own. Also returning to close games was John Wetteland, who had racked up 137 major league saves, 31 of them the previous season.

Catcher Mike Stanley had opted for free agency and defected to the hated Boston Red Sox. In his place was Joe Girardi, known more for his defense and his baseball smarts than for his bat (while Stanley had hit 61 homers and driven in 224 runs for the Yankees in the previous three seasons, Girardi was hitting 15 homers and driving in 120 runs for the Colorado Rockies). It was Girardi's defense, his deft handling of a pitching staff, and his leadership that prompted venerable coach Don Zimmer, who had managed him with the Chicago Cubs a few years earlier, to urge the Yankees to acquire Girardi.

Making a concession to his chronic back pain, Don Mattingly had retired and would be replaced at first base by Tino Martinez. Free agent Mariano Duncan was the new second baseman in place of injury-plagued Pat Kelly.

In short, what the Yankees had was a solid professional at just about every position. What they did not have was a shortstop. Veteran Tony Fernandez, their incumbent at the position, had broken his elbow in spring training, causing the Yankees to begin scouring the major leagues in search of a shortstop they might sign as a free agent or acquire in a trade.

The search led to the Seattle Mariners, who were willing to part with their backup shortstop, Felix Fermin. Fermin was not much of a hitter, but he was considered a wizard in the field, and defense was the Yankees' main priority at the position. They (i.e., the owner) believed the team had enough offense to carry Fermin's weak bat and were ready to make the deal. All it would take to get him, said the Mariners, was this rookie pitcher…this kid from Panama…um…what's his name? Mario…er, Mariano…Rivers…er, Rivera?

Two decades later everybody wants to take credit for being in favor of giving Jeter the starting shortstop job in 1996, but back then many were adhering to the age-old bromide that conventional wisdom preaches that you can't win with a rookie shortstop. Some even were convinced Jeter was better suited for the outfield than he was for shortstop and thought of him as the team's center fielder of the future.

WADE BOGGS

The lasting image of Wade Boggs as a Yankee is of him sitting astride a New York Police Department horse and galloping around the warning track at Yankee Stadium after the Yanks clinched the 1996 World Series.

After 11 seasons as a member of the Boston Red Sox and one of the most despised of all Yankees villains, Boggs became a Yankee in 1993 via free agency. He spent five years in Yankees pinstripes, batting .313 over that span and collecting 702 hits while batting .302, .342, .324, .311, and, at age 39, .292.

Boggs' overall major league record included 3,010 hits, a lifetime batting average of .328, five batting championships, and seven 200-hit seasons. He was inducted into the Baseball Hall of Fame in 2005.

In his playing days, Boggs was known for his superstitions and eccentricities. He ate chicken before every game, woke up at the same time every day, took 117 ground balls—no more, no less—during pregame practice, took batting practice at precisely 5:17 PM and ran sprints at precisely 7:17 PM.

In fact, the Yankees had not had a rookie open their season at shortstop since Tom Tresh in 1962, and then only because their regular shortstop, Tony Kubek, was fulfilling his military obligation.

But now, 34 years later, the decision was new manager Joe Torre's to make and he's on record for having penciled in the 21-year-old kid from Kalamazoo as the team's Opening Day shortstop.

"Starting with a new ballclub, in a new league, the one thing I knew was Derek Jeter was going to be my shortstop," recalled Joe Torre. "He didn't have a spectacular spring [although he batted a respectable .288, Jeter drove in only six runs, struck out 17 times, and made six errors in 23 games], but then Opening Day in Cleveland he hits a home run [off Dennis Martinez in the fifth inning in his second at-bat with the Yankees leading 1–0], makes a great catch [an over-the-shoulder grab on a pop-fly in short left field hit by Omar Vizquel], and it got to the point where I trusted him. Certainly in my mind he was older than his years."

For Torre, the defining moment, the event that earned Jeter the manager's confidence, came in Chicago on August 12 of that first year. The Yankees were tied 2–2 with the White Sox and batting in the eighth inning. With one out, Jeter singled and then moved to second on an infield out. Paul O'Neill was walked intentionally, putting Yankees on first and second with two outs and Cecil Fielder coming to bat.

"Normally the rule is you don't get thrown out at third base for the third or first out of an inning," Torre said. "Cecil Fielder, my cleanup hitter, is hitting, so give him a chance to hit! All of a sudden I see Jeter take off from second. It's all right if he's safe, but he was out.

"I'm sitting next to my bench coach, [Don] Zimmer, and I'm livid. I'm not sure who I'm mad at. I'm mad at Jeter and I'm mad at myself because I could have said don't try to steal; I could have given him a sign. I said to Zim, 'I'm not going to talk to him now because I don't want to ruffle his feathers. We have a couple of innings to play and he may come up to hit and I don't want to make him nervous.'

"Jeter had to stay in the field after he was thrown out. Somebody brought him his glove. The bottom half of the eighth is over and I see Derek Jeter jogging in off the field. Normally, he'd sit at the end of the bench, but this time he came right over at me and sat between Zimmer and myself as if to say, 'Okay, give me my punishment.' I hit him in the back of the head and said, 'Get out of here.'

"That told me this kid was special as far as being responsible at a young age. And then by the end of the year, it was very gratifying for me to see the Paul O'Neills, the Tino Martinezes, the Bernie Williamses, guys who have been around the block a day or two, to really start relying on this youngster, waiting for him to do something to lead the way."

And lead the way Jeter did. He played in 157 of the Yankees 162 games, batted .314, scored 104 runs, had 183 hits, 25 doubles, six triples, 10 home runs, 78 runs batted in, 14 stolen bases, an on-base percentage of .370, a slugging percentage of .430, and a fielding percentage of .969. He also received all 28 first-place votes for American League Rookie of the Year, cast by the Baseball Writers Association of America.

In his second big league season, Andy Pettitte improved by nine games over his rookie season and led the American League in wins. But Pettitte, at 21–8, was beaten out for the American League Cy Young Award by Pat Hentgen of the Toronto Blue Jays, who was 20–10, but had a lower ERA, more complete games, more shutouts, and more strikeouts.

In his first year as manager of the Yankees, Torre saw the light that apparently blinded Buck Showalter the year before and made Mariano Rivera his primary set-up man to closer John Wetteland, who saved 43 games, and there were many who insisted that Rivera was the Yankees' most valuable player in 1996. He won eight games, lost only three, had an earned run average of 2.09, and 130 strikeouts in 107⅔ innings. As a sign of things to come, Rivera even got a chance to close games when Wetteland was unavailable and picked up the first five saves of his career. There would be hundreds more.

His numbers were so dominant that Rivera finished ahead of Wetteland in both the American League Most Valuable Player and Cy Young voting.

There is a school of thought that promulgates the theory that in that one season, Rivera revolutionized the game of baseball, in particular how a team's bullpen is constructed and deployed today. He was so dominant setting up for Wetteland and pitching one, two, sometimes even three innings (he averaged 1.76 innings per appearance), that he personally shortened the game. It elevated the importance and, yes, the value of the set-up man and gave other teams the idea to emulate the practice.

The one member of the Core Four who did not make a significant contribution to the Yankees surge in 1996 was Jorge Posada, who became a frequent passenger on the Columbus-New York-Columbus shuttle. With Joe Girardi getting most of the work at catcher, and Posada in need of more experience at his new position, Jorge spent most of the season in Columbus, where he batted .271, hit 11 homers, and drove in 62 runs in 106 games while improving his defensive skills. He did make four trips to the Yankees and appeared in eight games, but had only one hit, a single, in 14 at-bats, a batting average of .071.

But Jorge Posada was still only 25 years old and his time had not yet come.

10   CHAMPS TO THE CORE

DEREK JETER'S ROOKIE YEAR AND JOE TORRE'S FIRST AS YANKEES
manager coincided in 1996. By that point the Yankees had gone
15 years without winning a pennant and 18 years without winning
the World Series, so it was considered merely more of the same
mediocrity when they split their first 12 games and fell 4½ games
out of first place in a formidable division that included the defending American League East champion Boston Red Sox and the still
powerful Baltimore Orioles.

But the Yankees would win seven of their next 11 games and
poke their nose ahead of the field in the American League East. By
July 28, they were 23 games over .500 and a whopping 12 games
ahead of the pack. A six-week malaise in August and September
saw the Yankees lose 23 of 39 games and their lead shrivel to just
2½ games. But faced with impending doom and a monumental
collapse, the Yankees righted the ship in time to win eight of their
final 14 games and finish four games ahead of the Orioles.

It was a major triumph for their first-year manager, made possible in large part not only by contributions from youngsters Andy
Pettitte (21 wins), Mariano Rivera (8–3 record), Derek Jeter (.314
average), but by veterans Tino Martinez (a .292 average, 25 homers,

and 117 RBI), Bernie Williams (.305, 29, 102), Paul O'Neill (.302, 19, 91), John Wetteland (43 saves), and pitchers Kenny Rogers, Doc Gooden, and Jimmy Key, who combined for 35 wins.

With their ouster by the Seattle Mariners in the first round the year before, and the fallout after losing that series by the removal of manager Buck Showalter fresh in their minds, the Yankees took on the Texas Rangers in the League Division Series. The Rangers, managed by former Yankee Johnny Oates, had been powered to the American League West title by slugger Juan Gonzalez, who belted 47 home runs and drove in 144 runs. To add to the Yanks' unease, John Burkett out-pitched David Cone and the Rangers took Game 1 of the best-of-five series 6–2 at Yankee Stadium.

When the Rangers scored a run in the second inning and Gonzalez blasted a three-run homer off Andy Pettitte in the third inning of Game 2 for a 4–1 lead, the huge stadium was shrouded in gloom with the thought that the Yankees would be going to Texas down two games to none.

But Cecil Fielder homered in the fourth, Charlie Hayes hit a sacrifice fly in the seventh, and Fielder tied the score with a single in the eighth. Meanwhile, Mariano Rivera, John Wetteland, Graeme Lloyd, Jeff Nelson, Kenny Rogers, and Brian Boehringer combined for 5⅔ scoreless innings and the Yankees batted in the bottom of the 12th with the score tied 4–4 and Jeter scheduled to be the Yankees' first batter.

Confirming Torre's assessment that he's special, Jeter led off with a single, his third hit of the game, and moved to second on a base on balls to Tim Raines. Jeter then scored when third baseman Dean Palmer threw Charlie Hayes' bunt wildly past first baseman Will Clark. Game over! The Yankees had dodged a bullet with the 5–4 victory and the series shifted to Texas, tied at one game apiece.

In Game 3, the Yankees once again found themselves backed against a wall, down 2–1 going to the top of the ninth, and once again Jeter, moved up from the ninth batting position to lead off, started the inning with a single, his second hit of the game. He went to third on Raines' single and scored the tying run on Bernie Williams' sacrifice fly. Raines reached second when Fielder grounded out and the Rangers intentionally walked Martinez to face Mariano Duncan, who had been an important player all season both on the field and as an inspirational leader.

Thirty-three years old and in his 11th major league season, Duncan was used sparingly by Torre in deference to his age. But he produced mightily, with eight home runs and 56 RBI in 109 games, a team-leading .340 average, and the creation of the slogan that would become the Yankees' rallying cry for the season. Duncan would arrive each day in the Yankees' clubhouse and shout for all to hear, "We play today; we win today!"

Now in the top of the ninth, Duncan put his bat where his mouth was and singled home Raines to put the Yankees ahead 3–2. Wetteland worked a scoreless bottom of the ninth and the Yankees were up two games to one.

The Rangers started off swinging in Game 4, with two runs in the second and two more in the third, one of them on Gonzalez's fifth home run of the series, for a 4–0 lead. Once again the Yankees were forced to come from behind. They began their comeback with a three-run rally in the fourth on four singles, two walks, a stolen base, and Jeter's RBI on a fielder's choice, tying it in the fifth on Bernie Williams' home run.

After Kenny Rogers and Brian Boehringer were tagged for four runs and eight hits over the first three innings, David Weathers, Mariano Rivera, and John Wetteland combined to hold the Rangers to one hit, three walks, and no runs over the final six innings. The Yankees took the lead in the seventh on Fielder's RBI single and Williams' second home run of the game gave them an insurance run in the ninth for a 6–4 win that knocked out the Rangers and sent the Yankees to the American League Championship Series against Baltimore.

The pattern that had been established in the division series—the Yankees falling behind early, their starting pitchers keeping them close, the bullpen coming in to shut down the opposition, the Yanks' bats heating up late in the game to overcome a deficit—continued in the League Championship Series.

Andy Pettitte started Game 1 and gave up single runs in the second, third, fourth, and sixth, leaving after seven innings with the Yanks behind 4–3. With one out in the bottom of the eighth, Jeter hit a line drive toward the right-field stands that was caught by a 12-year-old fan. The Orioles argued that right fielder Tony Tarasco would have caught the drive had the fan, Jeffrey Maier, not leaned his glove over the wall to catch the ball. Right-field umpire Richie Garcia decided Maier did not interfere with Tarasco and called it a home run, tying the score at 4–4.

Once more the Yankees' bullpen of Nelson, Wetteland, and Rivera held the opponents scoreless over the final four innings, and the Yankees won 5–4 on another home run by Bernie Williams leading off the bottom of the 11th inning.

After the Orioles won Game 2 by a score of 5–3, the series moved to Baltimore, where the Yankees would sweep three games from the Orioles, 5–2, 8–4, and 6–4, and move on the World Series against the defending World Series–champion Atlanta Braves. The Braves were currently in the process of putting together a dynasty, having won five division titles and reaching the World Series for the fourth time in the last six years. The Braves were led by Chipper Jones (.309, 30 home runs, 110 RBI), Fred McGriff (.295, 28, 107), Ryan Klesko (.282, 34, 93), and Javier Lopez (.282, 23, 69). But it was their pitching staff, including John Smoltz (24–8), Tom Glavine (15–10), Greg Maddux (15–11), and Mark Wohlers (39 saves) that really drove them.

First, Smoltz and four relievers held the Yankees to four hits in a 12–1 rout in Game 1, powered by two home runs from 19-year-old Andruw Jones and one by McGriff. Then, Maddux and Wohlers combined on a 4–0, seven-hit shutout in Game 2. Just like that the Braves had taken the first two games in Yankee Stadium. And, with the next three games to be played in Atlanta, you couldn't find anyone who gave the Yankees a snowball's chance in Georgia in this World Series.

Well, there was one.

Visited in the manager's office by a steaming and dejected George Steinbrenner after the second game, Joe Torre boldly predicted that the Yankees would win the World Series. Not only that, he said they would sweep the next four games.

Was this just false bravado? Was Torre merely whistling past the graveyard, putting on a brave front, making a preemptive strike against the man who controlled his professional fate and who had a penchant for replacing managers with very little provocation? Or did Torre have a premonition?

We'll never know why Torre made such a bold prediction. What we do know is that Torre's prediction was dead-on accurate.

Back in Atlanta's Fulton County Stadium, David Cone outpitched Tom Glavine in Game 3 and the Yankees won 5–2. Game 4, the following night, Wednesday, October 23, would follow the familiar pattern established in the previous playoff series, the Yankees falling behind early, their bullpen stifling the opponents' bats, the Yanks rallying from behind. Game 4 would prove to be the turning point of the World Series.

Down 6–0, the Yankees scored three runs in the top of the sixth, the rally started (surprise!) with a single by Jeter. But the Braves still held a 6–3 lead in the eighth when the Yankees put two runners on. The Braves' failure to succesfully turn what should have been a double play would be the huge break the Yankees needed, bringing Jim Leyritz to the plate. Leyritz had gone in to catch after Joe Girardi left for a pinch hitter and now here he was, the tying run, facing off against Mark Wohlers, the Braves' lockdown closer and his 100 mph fastball.

The count went to 2–2 when Leyritz fouled off two blistering fastballs, which must have convinced Wohlers to abandon his 100 mph heater with his next offering and switch to his second-best pitch, a slider. Wohlers had to be thinking that Leyritz certainly was expecting another fastball and the slider would catch him off guard. Wohlers' plan backfired. Leyritz jumped on the slider, drilling it over the left-field wall. The score was tied, but the Braves, for all practical purposes, were beaten.

While Yankees relievers Nelson, Rivera, Lloyd, and Wetteland were holding the Braves to three hits and no runs over the final five innings, the Yankees would finally break through with two runs in the 10th. The rally started with a two-out walk to Tim Raines, followed by an infield single by Jeter (again!).

The Yankees went up three games to two, completing a sweep of the three games in Atlanta when they won Game 5. This was the game in which Andy Pettitte first earned recognition as a big-game pitcher by outdueling Smoltz in a 1–0 victory.

Back at Yankee Stadium for Game 6, the Yankees scored three runs in the third on a double by Paul O'Neill, a triple by Joe Girardi, Jeter's single and stolen base, and Bernie Williams' RBI single. Jimmy Key and four relievers held the Braves to one run until the ninth, when Wetteland gave up singles to Terry Pendleton, Ryan Klesko, and Marquis Grissom for a run before getting Mark Lemke to pop to third baseman Charlie Hayes to nail down the Yankees' first World Series championship since 1978.

For three members of the Core Four it would be the first of several rides through New York City's Canyon of Heroes in lower Manhattan, and they had earned it with outstanding performances in the postseason.

Andy Pettitte was 1–0 in the League Championship Series and 1–1 in the World Series.

Mariano Rivera pitched 14⅓ innings in the postseason, won one game, lost none, and struck out 10.

Derek Jeter batted .412 in the Division Series with an RBI and two runs scored, .417 in the League Championship Series with a home run, an RBI, and five runs scored, and .250 in the World Series with an RBI and five runs scored.

Joe Torre had won his first World Series. Never again would he be called "Clueless Joe."

11 POSADA'S TIME

WHILE THE CAREERS OF MARIANO RIVERA, ANDY PETTITTE, AND Derek Jeter were flourishing, Jorge Posada's had been at a standstill, his rise delayed by Joe Girardi and by his own inexperience.

On December 5, 1996, Jim Leyritz, who had hit the biggest home run of the 1996 World Series, a game-tying, three-run shot in Game 4, was traded to the Anaheim Angels. Leyritz had caught 55 games as backup to Girardi while hitting .264 with seven home runs and 40 RBI. It was apparent that Leyritz was being traded to clear the way for Posada to finally say "Goodbye Columbus" and farewell to the Columbus-New York-Columbus shuttle and take up secure residence in the Bronx as Girardi's backup.

Still technically a rookie, Posada, on the strength of a .357 average, two home runs, and 11 RBI in spring training, was voted the James P. Dawson Award winner, named for the late *New York Times* baseball writer and Yankees correspondent, and presented annually since 1956 to the Yankees' outstanding rookie player in camp. When the major league season opened, Posada was on the Yankees' roster, the only rookie so rewarded.

Used mainly as Girardi's backup and as part of a platoon, Posada appeared in 60 games, 52 as the starting catcher, batted .250, hit six home runs, and drove in 25 runs.

The 1997 Yankees, led on offense by three players who would hit more than 21 homers and reach triple digits in RBI (Tino Martinez 44, 141, Paul O'Neill 21, 117, Bernie Williams 21, 100), were essentially the same team that had won the World Series the previous year, Joe Torre's first as manager. There was one notable exception.

Reliever John Wetteland, who had led the league with 43 saves in 1996, had gained free agency, and rather than pony up big dollars to keep him, the Yankees saw a chance to save money and, at the same time, reward one of their young lions. Convinced that Mariano Rivera was ready and able to step in and take over the closer's role, they let Wetteland walk and sign a four-year, $23 million contract with the Texas Rangers.

On April 15, Major League Baseball staged Jackie Robinson Day in every ballpark, commemorating the 50th anniversary of the day Robinson broke baseball's color barrier, while at the same time memorializing the 25th anniversary of his death. As part of the ceremonies, the commissioner's office decreed that henceforth no player would wear Robinson's No. 42. However, all those already wearing the number were granted a grandfather clause permitting them to wear the number for the remainder of their careers. That day there were 12 major league players who wore No. 42, including Rivera. In the 2012 season, he was the only one of the 12 still playing.

Rivera didn't disappoint in his new role as closer. He won six games and saved 43, two fewer than league-leader Randy Myers of the Baltimore Orioles, and the exact number that Wetteland had saved for the Yankees the season before (in his first season with the Rangers, Wetteland would win seven games and save 31).

The Yankees' 96 wins—while two more than the 1996 champs— were only enough for second place in the American League East, two games behind the Baltimore Orioles. New York's record was good enough, however, to qualify them for the postseason as the American League wild-card team.

Paired against the AL Central–champion Cleveland Indians in the 1997 Division Series, the Yankees found themselves behind early when the Indians scored five runs in the first inning of Game 1 at Yankee Stadium. The Yankees rallied from behind, got home runs from O'Neill, Martinez, Derek Jeter, and Tim Raines, scored five runs in the sixth to take the lead, and won 8–6 with Rivera pitching an inning and a third for his first postseason save.

The Indians turned the tables in Game 2, watching the Yankees score three times in the first and then coming back for a 7–5 win to tie the series at one game each.

Game 3 in Cleveland was all New York. O'Neill, an Ohio native, hit another homer, and David Wells pitched a complete-game five-hitter for a 6–1 victory that put the Yankees up two games to one in the best-of-five series, one win away from advancing to the American League Championship Series and two chances to get it.

The Yankees jumped out to a 2–0 lead in the first inning of Game 4. The Indians got one run back in the second, but starter Dwight Gooden and a tag team of relievers—Graeme Lloyd, Jeff Nelson, and Mike Stanton—preserved the lead into the eighth when, with one out, Rivera came in for what would be a five-out save. He retired the first batter, Matt Williams, a right-handed hitter, on a fly ball to right fielder O'Neill. The next batter, Sandy Alomar Jr., took two pitches out of the strike zone and then teed off on Rivera's cutter and, like Williams, drove it to right field. Unlike Williams, Alomar's ball reached the fences and beyond to tie the score 2–2.

The Indians would push across a run in the ninth on Omar Vizquel's RBI single and the series was tied, two games each, with the sudden-death fifth game to be played the following night in Cleveland.

The Indians jumped out to an early lead with a three-run third against Andy Pettitte, added a run in the fourth, and held on as the

Yankees scored two in the fifth and one in the sixth, but left two runners on base in the eighth and one in the ninth, and were defeated 4–3.

Posada appeared in two games against the Indians, batting twice without a hit. But it was becoming apparent that barring a trade for a big name (always a possibility with the Yankees), Posada was being groomed to take over as the team's No. 1 catcher. He was seven years younger than Girardi, had more power, and was a switch-hitter, which made him a left-handed threat in Yankee Stadium's short right-field porch.

BERNIE WILLIAMS

Often referred to as the fifth member of the Core Four, Bernie Williams signed with the Yankees as an amateur free agent out of San Juan, Puerto Rico, in 1985, and reached Yankee Stadium in 1991, four years before the arrival of Mariano Rivera, Andy Pettitte, Jorge Posada, and Derek Jeter. Except for the time Pettitte spent in Houston, the five would play together as teammates for the rest of Williams' 16-year career, all with the Yankees, and win six pennants and four World Series championships.

For his career, Williams posted Hall of Fame numbers: a .297 batting average, 2,336 hits, 287 home runs, and 1,257 runs batted in. The latest in a long line of superstar Yankee center fielders, Williams is sixth on the Yankees all-time list in games played, fourth in at-bats, sixth in runs, fifth in hits, third in doubles, seventh in home runs, sixth in RBIs, and 16th in batting average. He was a five-time All-Star, as well as the 1998 American League–batting champion with a .339 average. Five times he drove in at least 100 runs and he reached double figures in home runs for 14 consecutive seasons.

Williams never officially announced his retirement from baseball, but since playing his last major league game he has forged
a successful second career as an accomplished classical and jazz
guitarist and composer. When the enormously popular Williams attended ceremonies before the final game at the old Yankee Stadium,
he received an ovation that lasted one minute and 42 seconds.

By 1998, Posada's time had come. Some observers thought it
was a year late, that Girardi held on to the starting job because
he had a staunch and loyal ally in bench coach Don Zimmer,
who campaigned strongly in Girardi's behalf. But when Posada
slammed three hits, including a home run, in the fourth game of
the season and came back with two hits, including another home
run, in the sixth game of the season, manager Joe Torre adjusted
his plans.

No longer was Posada considered a defensive liability. He had
earned Torre's trust with his improvement behind the plate, and for
the first time he got more calls as the starting catcher than Girardi
85–76. But it was the potential of his bat that made Posada a more
attractive option than an aging and fading Girardi. Posada would
prove to be a potent addition to a team that would win a franchise
record 114 games and finish 22 games ahead of the second-place
Boston Red Sox in the American League East. Although out-hit
by Girardi .276 to .268, Posada had a huge edge in home runs (17
to 3) and RBI (63 to 31), and was rewarded with more playing
time than Girardi in the postseason.

Many believe the 1998 Yankees to be the greatest of all Yankees
teams. Certainly they belong in the conversation with the 1927,
1936, 1939, and 1961 Yankees.

Bernie Williams, American League batting champion at .339,
was one of four Yankees in 1998 with a batting average of .300 or

better. The others were Derek Jeter (.324), Paul O'Neill (.317), and Scott Brosius (.300), who came to the Yankees as the "player to be named later" in the deal that sent Kenny Rogers to Oakland, and whose lifetime batting average for seven seasons prior to coming to the Yankees was .248.

Four Yankees hit more than 20 home runs that season: Tino Martinez (28), Williams (26), and O'Neill and Darryl Strawberry (24). Jeter and Brosius each hit 19. Martinez (123) and O'Neill (116) each drove in more than 100 runs. Brosius knocked in 98. David Cone tied for the league lead in wins with 20. David Wells won 18 and Andy Pettitte 16. Three others had double figures in wins: Hideki Irabu (13), Orlando Hernandez (12), and Ramiro Mendoza (10). And Mariano Rivera, in his second year as Yankees' closer, had 36 saves and an earned run average of 1.91.

Just as they had done during the regular season, the Yankees ran roughshod over their opponents in the postseason, sweeping three games from the Texas Rangers in the Division Series, taking four out of six from the Cleveland Indians in the American League Championship Series, and sweeping the San Diego Padres to win their second World Series in three years and the 24th in their history.

Posada would appear in only one game in the Division Series and go hitless in two at-bats, but in the ALCS he was in five of the six games, started three of them, and had two hits in 11 at-bats, including his first postseason home run in Game 1. He started the first two games of the World Series, was 3-for-9 in the Series and hit another home run, a two-run shot in Game 2. And for the first time, Posada felt he truly belonged as the Yankees took another ride through Manhattan's Canyon of Heroes.

The 1999 season was a slight setback for Posada. His batting average dropped from .268 to .245, his home runs from 17 to 12, and his RBI from 63 to 57, but the Yankees won their third pennant and World Series in four years, and Posada looked forward to good times ahead.

Posada's joy in playing for the winning side in the World Series for the second straight year and third time in four years was more than matched by the joy he realized a few weeks later with the birth of his first child, Jorge Posada Jr., on November 28. But that joy was tempered and fear set in just 10 days later when Jorge and Laura Posada were informed that young Jorge was born with craniosynostosis, a rare pediatric deformity of the skull that occurs in one out of every 2,000 births when the bones in the child's skull fuse together before the brain has stopped growing.

Doctors told the Posadas that the condition could be corrected by multiple surgeries. The first surgery was an eight-hour procedure that Jorge Jr. underwent before his first birthday. There were eight more surgeries, and all the while Posada kept silent about his son's medical problems. The fact that he was able to carve out a potential Hall of Fame career while dealing with such personal stress is a tribute to his courage and his grit.

Eventually, the Posadas went public with their son's condition, which gave rise to the Miami-based Jorge Posada Foundation, an emotional and financial support group for families with a child afflicted with craniosynostosis.

Today, Jorge Posada Jr. is a normal teenager with no physical limitations.

In 1999, Posada pretty much took over the Yankees' full-time catcher's job, starting 98 games to Girardi's 64. Offensively, it was no contest. Posada out-hit Girardi .245 to .239, hit 12 homers to Girardi's two, and drove in 57 runs to Girardi's 27.

The Yankees won 98 games, but were pushed in the AL East by the Boston Red Sox, finally finishing 4½ games ahead of their New England rivals. For the second straight year the Yankees met the Texas Rangers in the Division Series and for the second straight year the Yankees handed the Rangers a shellacking, sweeping the three-game series by scores of 8–0, 3–1, and 3–0.

While the Yankees were disposing of Texas in three games, the

Red Sox were erasing the Cleveland Indians in five games, pitting the Yankees and Red Sox, the two archrivals, against each other in the ALCS. It took five games for the Yanks to get rid of the Sox. That set up a rematch of the 1996 World Series, the Yankees against the Atlanta Braves, who were eager to avenge their defeat of three years earlier. This time the Yankees made it quick, blitzing the Braves in a four-game sweep.

Posada and Girardi pretty much split time behind the plate for the Yankees in the 1999 postseason. Neither was particularly effective offensively. Girardi was a combined 4-for-21 for a .190 average, without a home run or a run batted in, and Posada was 4-for-22 for a .182 average, but did have a home run and three RBI.

A year later, Posada's situation would change dramatically, and for the better. Girardi left the Yankees (he attained free agency and signed with the Chicago Cubs, his first big league club and his hometown team), leaving Posada to do the bulk of the catching for the Yankees, with only cameo appearances from Chris Turner and Jim Leyritz. Posada would play in 151 games, 142 of them behind the plate, and he would have a breakout season. His .287 average, 28 home runs, and 86 RBI earned him his first All-Star selection and his first Silver Slugger Award, which is presented to the leading hitter at every defensive position in each league.

Although their win total slipped to 87, the Yankees held off the charge of the Boston Red Sox to finish first in the AL East by 2½ games. They would then beat the Oakland Athletics three games to two in the Division Series, the Seattle Mariners four games to two in the League Championship Series, and their crosstown rivals, the New York Mets, four games to one to win their third straight World Series (and their fourth in five years). Derek Jeter hit a quinella by being voted the Most Valuable Player in both the 2000 All-Star Game and the World Series.

In the three-year period from 1998 to 2000, the Yankees would attain postseason success the likes of which had never been seen before and likely never will be seen again. And the Core Four were important contributors to this unprecedented run.

In that stretch, the Yankees played 41 games and won 33 of them, a winning percentage of .805, phenomenal considering the high drama, excruciating pressure, intensity, and scrutiny under which the games were played. At one stage, they won 12 straight of these high-pressure games, and from Game 3 in 1996 to Game 2 in 2000 the Yankees won a ridiculous 14 World Series games in a row.

Posada played in 31 of those 41 games, contributed 20 hits, scored 11 runs, hit three home runs, and drove in 12 runs.

Pettitte pitched in 11 games, won six, and lost one.

Rivera was in 28 of the 41 games, with a 2–0 record. He also saved 18, allowed three earned runs in $41\frac{1}{3}$ innings for an ERA of 0.65, struck out 30, walked only three, and had a scoreless streak of $33\frac{1}{3}$ innings ended in the 2000 ALCS.

Jeter played in every inning of every one of the 41 games. He had 50 hits in 162 at-bats, a .309 average, stole seven bases, scored 30 runs, hit five home runs, and drove in 16.

12   SAY IT AIN'T SO, MO

ALL GOOD THINGS MUST END!

And so the Yankees' magical mystery tour through the major league postseason had its conclusion on Sunday night, November 4, 2001, in Phoenix's Bank One Ballpark. And it concluded in the most unusual, most unpredictable fashion, with Mariano Rivera, who had pitched in 51 postseason games without suffering a defeat and had rung up 23 consecutive postseason saves to that point, walking off the mound as a losing pitcher for the first (and to this date, only) time in 96 Division Series, League Championship Series, and World Series games.

The Yankees seemed headed inevitably for a fourth straight World Series championship after coming through, against all odds, a best-of-five League Division Series in which they lost the first two games at home. They then steamrolled the Seattle Mariners in five games in the best-of-seven American League Championship Series, and followed that up by scoring two improbable, sudden-death victories in the World Series against the Arizona Diamondbacks.

Few gave much for the Yankees' chances against the A's after Mark Mulder beat Roger Clemens 5–3 in Game 1 of the Division Series and Tim Hudson out-pitched Andy Pettitte 2–0 in Game

2. Not even the battle-tested, four-time World Series–champion never-say-die Yankees seemed capable of winning two games on the road and a sudden-death fifth game at home. And all this against an Oakland team rich in pitching and possessed of a potent offense that was headed by the Nos. 1, 3, and 5 hitters in their lineup: Johnny Damon, Jason Giambi, and Eric Chavez (all three of whom would eventually wear the Yankees pinstripes), who had combined for 308 runs, 79 home runs, and 283 RBI in the regular season.

Game 3 in Oakland changed everything. Mike Mussina was brilliant for seven innings in out-pitching Barry Zito, Mariano Rivera was his usual lockdown self for the final two innings, Jorge Posada belted a home run in the fifth inning, and Derek Jeter made a remarkable, spectacular, instinctive, game-saving, Series-saving play that would come to be known as "the Flip," in a pulsating 1–0 victory that enabled the Yankees to live to see another day.

Game 4 was a blowout, a 9–2 laugher, shifting the scene for the fifth game to Yankee Stadium and the momentum to the Yankees. Now there were few who *didn't* believe the Yankees would win the game and the Series and go on to capture the ALCS and the World Series.

Back home for Game 5, the Yanks sent Clemens to the mound against Mulder. Neither could get out of the fifth inning. When Clemens had a spate of wildness with one out in the fifth (a walk, a wild pitch, a hit batsman), he was replaced by Mike Stanton with the Yankees leading 4–2 and Clemens two outs away from qualifying for the victory. Mariano Rivera pitched two scoreless innings for his second save of the series. Jeter and Posada each batted .444 and had identical logs of eight hits in 18 at-bats.

The Yankees were moving on to the League Championship Series, where for the second straight year they would meet the Seattle Mariners, who were led to a record 116 victories by manager Lou Piniella, the former Yankee star player, manager, and general manager.

The series was no contest. The Yankees first did to the Mariners what the Athletics had done to the Yankees. They won the first two games on their opponent's field, 4–2 behind Pettitte in Game 1, and 3–2 behind Mussina in Game 2, with Rivera collecting a save in each game.

SCOTT BROSIUS

An average player in seven seasons with the Oakland Athletics, Scott Brosius was traded to the Yankees after the 1997 season and elbowed himself into the team's lore with one season and one home run. In 1998, his first year as a Yankee, he improved his batting average from .203 to .300, his home runs shot up from 11 to 19, and his RBIs from 41 to 98. He then followed that up by batting .471 in the World Series against the San Diego Padres, with two home runs and six runs batted in, for which he was voted the Series' Most Valuable Player.

Three years later, Brosius hit one of the most famous home runs in World Series history: Game 5 between the Yankees and Arizona Diamondbacks, bottom of the ninth, two outs, the Yankees down by two runs, a runner on base and Brosius batting against Diamondbacks' closer Byung-Hyun Kim. The night before, Tino Martinez had come to bat in a similar situation—two outs, bottom of the ninth, runner on base, the Yanks down by two runs, Byung-Hyun Kim on the mound—and hit a game-tying home run. And it happened again: same situation, same pitcher, different hitter. A two-run home run that sent the game into extra innings.

Brosius would quit while he was ahead. He retired after the World Series and returned to his Oregon home, where he is presently the baseball coach at his alma mater, Linfield College.

In Yankee Stadium for Game 3, the Mariners broke out with a 15-hit attack for a 14–3 victory, but unlike the Athletics, the Yankees did not cave in. They won Game 4 by a score of 3–1, and blasted the Mariners 12–3 in Game 5. Rivera got the win in Game 4. Pettitte, who would be voted the Most Valuable Player of the ALCS, was the winner of Game 5. Rivera pitched the ninth inning of the blowout in a non-save situation, manager Joe Torre's homage to his invincible closer by having him on the field when the Yankees clinched the 38th American League pennant in the team's history.

In the World Series the Yankees met a new opponent, the expansion Arizona Diamondbacks, in only the fourth year of their existence. They would prove to be a formidable opponent with an offense led by Luis Gonzalez, who hit 57 home runs and drove in 142 runs during the season. In most years those numbers would have led the league, but in 2001 Barry Bonds hit 73 homers and Sammy Sosa hit 64, and Sosa's 160 RBI was tops in the league.

The real strength of the 2001 Diamondbacks, however, was their starting pitching, bulwarked by the fearsome one-two punch of Curt Schilling (22–6) and Randy Johnson (21–6). Between them they had pitched 506⅓ innings and struck out 665 batters.

The first two games of the World Series in Arizona were right off the DBacks' drawing board. Schilling pitched seven overpowering innings in Game 1, allowed one run and three hits and struck out eight and Gonzalez hit a two-run home run in a four-run third in Arizona's 9–1 win. Randy Johnson went the distance in the second game, allowing three hits, striking out 11, and out-pitching Pettitte in a 4–0 victory. So here were the Yankees in a familiar position, down two games to none, just as they were against Oakland in the Division Series. The difference was this was a best-of-seven series and the Yanks would be the home team for the next three games.

The pregame pageantry of Game 3 of the World Series on the night of October 30, 2001, stirred emotions like never before. The customary red, white, and blue bunting that decorated Yankee Stadium never had such meaning. Exactly seven weeks to the day earlier, terrorists had leveled both towers of the World Trade Center, some 10 miles away in lower Manhattan, killing thousands and throwing the city, and the nation, into a panic and mourning.

In an effort to ease the tension, President George W. Bush, a lifelong baseball fan and a former owner of the Texas Rangers, accepted Major League Baseball's invitation to throw out the first pitch. Security in and around the stadium was tight, but the president would be vulnerable, standing alone and unprotected on the pitcher's mound. He would not, by his own choosing, be wearing the bulletproof vest that had been provided for him. The president was a baseball purist and he reasoned that the vest would interfere with his goal to throw a perfect strike to Yankees' backup catcher, Todd Greene.

To ensure his ability to make a good, strong pitch, the president arranged to take a few pregame warm-up, range-finding throws under the stands in the bowels of the Stadium. As he was taking his tosses, Derek Jeter walked by.

"Hey, Mr. President," said the captain of the Yankees without saluting the commander in chief. "Are you going to throw from the mound or from the front of it?"

"What do you think?" Bush replied.

"Throw from the mound or else they'll boo you," said Jeter who started walking away. Suddenly he stopped, looked back, and said, "But don't bounce it. They'll boo you."

The president didn't bounce the throw. He fired a perfect strike and headed triumphantly toward home plate. As he walked to greet, and be greeted by, Todd Greene and the two managers, Bob Brenly and Joe Torre, the huge crowd began to chant spontaneously "USA…USA…USA…"

Perhaps moved by the pregame ceremony or motivated to match what Schilling and Johnson had done in the first two games,

Roger Clemens, a man of enormous professional ego and pride and like President Bush a Texan, pitched brilliantly.

Posada had staked Clemens to a one-run lead with a home run in the bottom of the second, ending an 18-inning scoreless streak by the Yankees. The Diamondbacks tied the score in the fourth on Matt Williams' sacrifice fly, but the Yankees regained the lead in the sixth on a single by Bernie Williams, a walk, and Scott Brosius' RBI single. And that's how it ended, a 2–1 victory for the Yankees.

At the top of his game, Clemens, who left after the seventh, allowed just the one run and three hits while striking out nine. Rivera came in for a six-out save and retired the Diamondbacks in order in the eighth and ninth, four of the outs by strikeout. The Yankees had broken through with a victory and the fun was just beginning. The Yankee Stadium crowd, and the national television audience, had seen nothing yet.

Events of the next two nights in Yankee Stadium produced such high drama and excruciating tension that many who watched began calling the 2001 World Series among the greatest ever played.

Game 4 was a spectacular, if nail-biting, pitchers' duel between Schilling and Orlando "El Duque" Hernandez, a 1–1 tie after seven nerve-wracking innings.

The Diamondbacks pushed across two runs in the top of the eighth and turned the lead over to their Korean relief pitcher Byung-Hyun Kim, who had taken over as the team's closer at midseason and racked up 19 saves to go with his five wins. When Kim breezed through the bottom of the eighth with consecutive strikeouts of Shane Spencer, Scott Brosius, and Alfonso Soriano, the euphoria in the stadium from the emotional and stirring pre-game pageantry had turned to gloom.

In the bottom of the ninth, Jeter attempted to bunt his way on base. Reacting alertly, third baseman Matt Williams fielded the bunt and threw Jeter out at first. Paul O'Neill followed with a bloop single that gave a glimmer of hope to the hometown crowd, but their eager anticipation was dashed when Kim fanned Bernie Williams. That brought up Tino Martinez, the Yankees' last hope, who had grounded out, struck out, and walked in three previous plate appearances and was hitless in nine at-bats in the Series.

Martinez attacked Kim's first pitch and drove it into the autumn night, a majestic blast straightaway to center field, where it soared over the fence to tie the game at 3–3. Rivera retired the Diamondbacks in order in the top of the 10th and Kim disposed of Brosius and Soriano on fly balls in the bottom of the 10th to bring up Jeter, who had been in a 1-for-15 slide in the Series.

Kim jumped ahead 0–2 but couldn't put away Jeter, who fouled off four pitches while running the count to 3–2. Jeter offered at Kim's next pitch and with his trademark inside-out swing he sent a high drive toward the right-field corner, where right fielder Reggie Sanders could only watch as the ball sailed over his head and the wall and into the lower right-field seats.

The Yankees' improbable 4–3 victory sent the crowd of 55,863 into a frenzy and tied the World Series at two games a piece on an at-bat that literally spanned a month. Jeter had stepped into the batter's box on October 31, and the ball flew over the right-field fence at precisely 12:03 AM on November 1. Derek Jeter had a new nickname.

"Mr. November!"

It was only the third time in 97 World Series and 500 World Series games that a team won a game after trailing by at least two runs in the bottom of ninth inning.

Remarkably, only 24 hours later, it happened again.

The same two-run deficit as the night before, the same bottom of the ninth with two outs and a runner on base, the same Diamondback pitcher on the mound.

Déjà vu all over again, as Yogi Berra would say.

Mike Mussina for the Yankees and Miguel Batista for the Diamondbacks were the starting pitchers who dueled through seven anxious innings in Game 5. Arizona pushed across two runs in the fifth on home runs by Steve Finley and Rod Barajas as Batista held the Yankees scoreless.

It remained 2–0 going into the bottom of the ninth, when once again Kim was brought in to protect a two-run lead. Posada started the inning with a double, but Spencer grounded out and Knoblauch struck out, and for the second straight night Kim and the Diamondbacks were one out away from victory.

This time the batter was Scott Brosius, who had grounded out and flied out twice in three at-bats in this game and was 3-for-16 in the Series. With the count 1–0 Brosius drove Kim's pitch deep into the left-field seats to tie the score. Miraculously, the Yankees had done it again, and so had Byung-Hyan Kim.

They went to extra innings. Rivera pitched a scoreless 10th and 11th, then Sterling Hitchcock a perfect 12th. In the bottom of the 12th, Knoblauch singled, Brosius sacrificed, and Soriano singled to score Knoblauch with the winning run. The Yankees were going to Arizona up three games to two. They would have to win only one game of the two, but they would have to do it against Randy Johnson and Curt Schilling.

Johnson was not his usual overpowering self in Game 6 (he allowed two runs and six hits and struck out seven in seven innings), but he didn't have to be. The Diamondbacks beat up on Pettitte and crushed the Yankees 15–2.

So it would all come down to one final game, in Phoenix's Bank One Ballpark on Sunday night, November 4, Roger Clemens squaring off against Curt Schilling, a matchup of pitching heavyweights. The Yankees had one consolation. They wouldn't have to worry about facing Randy Johnson again. Or would they?

As advertised, Clemens and Schilling were at the top of their game as they dueled through five scoreless innings. The Diamondbacks pushed across a run in the bottom of the sixth on a single by Steve Finley and an RBI double by Danny Bautista,

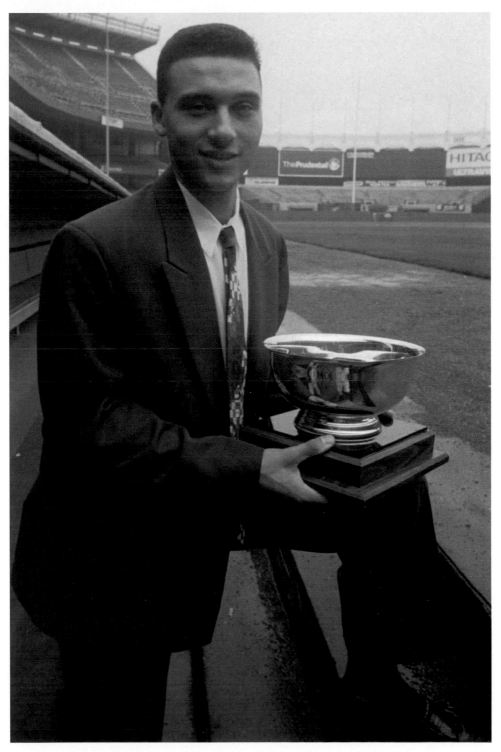

Derek Jeter on the dugout steps of Yankee Stadium on September 14, 1994, after he was named Baseball America's Minor League Player of the Year. *(AP Images)*

Rookie Andy Pettitte pitches against the Detroit Tigers in September 1995.

Mariano Rivera in 1996, the year in which he would record his first major league save.

Jorge Posada has a mound meeting with veteran pitcher David Wells during a May game in 1997, Jorge's rookie season.

Andy Pettitte celebrates with the World Series trophy after the Yankees defeated the Atlanta Braves four games to two in the 1996 Fall Classic. *(AP Images)*

Mariano Rivera and the Yankees celebrate after the final out of their four-game sweep over the San Diego Padres in the 1998 World Series.

Jorge Posada, Mariano Rivera, and Scott Brosius meet at the mound to celebrate sweeping the Atlanta Braves to win the 1999 World Series.

Jorge Posada and Andy Pettitte talk strategy during the seventh inning of Game 5 of the 2000 "Subway Series" against the Mets, which the Yankees would go on to win in five games. *(AP Images)*

and the Yankees tied it in the top of the seventh when Jeter singled to start a rally, went to second on O'Neill's single, to third on a ground-out, and scored on a Martinez single.

When Tony Womack singled with one out in the bottom of the seventh, Mike Stanton replaced Clemens, who left having allowed one run and seven hits with 10 strikeouts but with no chance to get a win. Posada threw Womack out attempting to steal second and Stanton retired Craig Counsell on a foul pop to first.

Soriano led off the top of the eighth with a home run off Schilling to give the Yankees a 2–1 lead. Schilling left on the losing end, replaced by Miguel Batista, who got Jeter to hit into a force play. With the left-handed hitting O'Neill due up, Brenly removed Batista and brought in Johnson, pitching for the second straight day. Torre countered by replacing O'Neill with the right-handed hitting Knoblauch, who flied to right to end the inning.

Johnson would face four batters and retire each one, but with a one-run lead, the Yankees were in great shape. They had Mariano Rivera, and Joe Torre called on him to nail down another world championship for the Yankees with a two-inning save.

In the eighth Rivera struck out Gonzalez, Williams, and Bautista around a single by Finley. With one more scoreless inning by the incomparable Rivera, the Yankees would win their fourth straight World Series.

Even when Mark Grace opened the bottom of the ninth with a single, there was no reason for concern. But what happened next might have been viewed as a bad omen for the Yankees. Asked to sacrifice the tying run to second, Damian Miller dropped an ineffectual bunt that was fielded by Rivera, as deft a fielder as he is dominant a pitcher. With a chance to force David Dellucci, pinch-running for Grace, Rivera fired wildly past Jeter at second for a rare error and the DBacks had the tying run on second and the winning run on first with no outs.

Jay Bell, pinch-hitting for Johnson, was called on to bunt the runners along. Like Miller, he bunted back to Rivera and this time Mariano threw a perfect strike to third baseman Brosius to force Dellucci, leaving runners on first and second but now with one out. A double play would end it and give the Yankees the Series, but Womack shockingly drove a pitch into the right field corner for a double. Midre Cummings, running for Miller, scored the tying run and Bell raced to third with the winning run.

Craig Counsell, the next batter, was hit by a pitch (was the usually composed Rivera coming unglued?) to load the bases and that brought up the Diamondbacks' leading hitter and biggest threat, Luis Gonzalez. With no place to put him, Rivera had to pitch to the Diamondbacks most dangerous hitter.

Because a long fly would score the winning run, the outfield was drawn in, but so, too, was the infield, the objective obviously being to cut the winning run off at the plate. Rivera went to work on Gonzalez and threw him his signature cut fastball, which had the usual result of breaking the hitter's bat. Unfortunately for the Yankees, Gonzalez was strong enough to muscle the ball to center field, too far out for the drawn in infield to reach it and not out far enough for the drawn in outfield to reach it.

Jay Bell scored from third as the Diamondbacks won their first World Series and the Yankees were denied their 27th World Series title.

As the jubilant Diamondbacks and their joyous fans celebrated this unprecedented and unexpected triumph, a disheartened, lonely figure could be seen walking disconsolately off the field at the conclusion of the World Series. For Mariano Rivera it was something he had never before experienced.

13 OH CAPTAIN, MY CAPTAIN

FOR MORE THAN 100 YEARS THE STEREOTYPE FOR THE MAJOR LEAGUE shortstop was an undersized, speedy, agile singles hitter—with one notable exception, Honus Wagner the legendary "Flying Dutchman of the Pittsburgh Pirates—such as Hall of Famers Phil Rizzuto (5'6", 150 pounds), Luis Aparicio (5'9", 155), Ozzie Smith (5'11", 150), Pee Wee Reese (5'9½", 165), Rabbit Maranville (5'5", 155), Joe Sewell (5'7", 160), Davey Bancroft (5'9", 160), and Joe Tinker (5'9", 175).

By the 1990s, major league shortstops, like people everywhere, were growing bigger and stronger. The first acknowledged superstar shortstop to break the mold, and the stereotype, was the Baltimore Orioles' Iron Man, Cal Ripken Jr., who, at an imposing 6'4" and 225 pounds, was built more like a home run–hitting third baseman, first baseman, or outfielder. A few years later, in the mid-1990s, a cadre of talented young shortstops arrived in the American League, the likes of which had never before been seen.

In 1996, in his third major league season (his first full season), 20-year-old Alex Rodriguez of the Seattle Mariners, 6'3" and 225 pounds, hit 36 home runs, drove in 123 runs, batted an American League–leading .358, made the All-Star team and was second in Most Valuable Player voting.

That same season, 22-year-old Derek Jeter of the New York Yankees, 6'3" and 195 pounds, batted .314, hit 10 home runs, knocked in 78 runs, and was voted American League Rookie of the Year.

In 1997, 23-year-old Nomar Garciaparra of the Boston Red Sox, 6' and 165 pounds, in his second major league season (he had played in 24 games the previous year) hit 30 home runs, drove in 98 runs, made the All-Star team, and was voted American League Rookie of the Year.

In 1999, 25-year-old Miguel Tejada of the Oakland Athletics, 5'9" and 220 pounds, belted 21 homers and drove in 84 runs.

No longer was the shortstop the runt of the major league litter.

To be sure, people living at the end of the 20th century and the beginning of the 21st century, by virtue of improved diet, better health care, greater knowledge of the body, and a conscious effort to live healthier lives, are bigger, stronger, and more physically active than their forebears, yet it is difficult to conjure up the fact that Jeter is taller than Babe Ruth, Lou Gehrig, Joe DiMaggio, Mickey Mantle, Roger Maris, Reggie Jackson, Don Mattingly, Bill Dickey, and Yogi Berra, and heavier than DiMaggio, Mattingly, and Berra.[1]

In his first eight full major league seasons, Jeter played in six World Series, four of them on the winning side, made the All-Star team five times, batted over .300 six times, and became established as one of baseball's best players and true leaders.

In recognition of his leadership, his competitiveness, his dependability, the respect he had from teammates and opponents, Yankees owner George Steinbrenner, seeking a solution to a malaise that had seen his team lose 12 of 15 games and fall into second place the previous month, announced on June 3, 2003, that Jeter was being named the 11th captain in the Yankees history. It's

---

1 Weights and measures courtesy of BaseballReference.com.

an honor for a Yankee almost as great as having one's number permanently retired, and a distinction that had been held by an imposing list of Yankees heroes of the past, including Hal Chase, Babe Ruth, Lou Gehrig, Thurman Munson, Graig Nettles, Willie Randolph, Ron Guidry, and Don Mattingly. The Yankees captaincy had been vacant since Mattingly retired eight years earlier.

Once before, Steinbrenner had shown the esteem he had for the position. At the start of the 1976 season, he announced that Munson was being named captain, filling a position that had been vacant for 36 years, following the death of Gehrig. When it was pointed out to Steinbrenner that at the time of Gehrig's death manager Joe McCarthy said out of respect for Gehrig the Yankees would never have another captain, the Boss replied, "If Joe McCarthy knew Thurman Munson, he'd agree this was the right guy and the right time."

But why Derek Jeter? And why now? Again, Steinbrenner had an answer.

"I think he can hopefully pull them together. I think he can give them a little spark. I just feel it's the right time to do it. People may say, 'What a time to pick.' Well, why not? He represents all that is good about a leader. I'm a great believer in history, and I look at all the other leaders down through Yankee history, and Jeter is right there with them."

To Jeter, the honor was appreciated, but he made certain to emphasize that the role was not going to change him; it was not going to make him more motivated, more determined, or more focused.

"He just says he wants me to be a leader, like I have been," Jeter said. "The impression I got is just continue to do the things I have been doing."

It was also significant that the announcement came just a few months after Jeter clashed with the Boss, who questioned the shortstop's off-field lifestyle, of all things. Steinbrenner mentioned that Jeter had been out at a birthday party until 3:00 AM during the 2002 season and wondered if Jeter might have lost his focus and if his lifestyle was suspect. It was a shocking accusation because Jeter had never had even the hint of a scandal of any sort in almost a decade with the Yankees.

Instead of pulling apart the owner and his best player, it served to bring them closer together. Jeter heard what Steinbrenner was saying, got the message, and made a concerted effort not to do anything that would call his lifestyle into question. Jeter and Steinbrenner even got together to film an amusing and award-winning commercial for Visa that alluded to the shortstop's off-field activities.

A decade has passed since Steinbrenner's rant against Jeter without the slightest hint that Jeter's decorum off the field is anything but above reproach.

Almost two decades have passed since the Fabulous Four shortstops arrived on the scene in the American League. Of the four, Garciaparra and Tejada are retired and Rodriguez has moved to another position.

Only Jeter remains at the same old stand, adding each year to his monumental list of achievements. For instance, as of the end of the 2012 season:

He has hit more home runs as a Yankee than Graig Nettles, Don Mattingly, Roger Maris, Bill Dickey, Tino Martinez, Paul O'Neill, Charlie Keller, Tommy Henrich, and Bobby Murcer.

He has a higher lifetime batting average as a Yankee than Bob Meusel, Don Mattingly, Ben Chapman, Mickey Mantle, Bernie Williams, Lou Piniella, and Willie ("Hit 'em where they ain't") Keeler.

He has more doubles as a Yankee than every other player except Gehrig.

He has more triples as a Yankee than Phil Rizzuto.

He has scored more runs as a Yankee than every other player except Ruth and Gehrig.

He has driven in more runs as a Yankee than Bill Dickey, Tony Lazzeri, Roy White, and Elston Howard.

He has played in more games, had more hits, more at-bats, and stolen more bases as a Yankee than any other player.

14　BOONE OR BUST

WINNING FIVE CONSECUTIVE DIVISION CHAMPIONSHIPS WOULD BE enough to cause most major league teams to rejoice.

Not the New York Yankees!

For them, no season could be a success unless they won the World Series.

So consider the years 2002 through 2006 failures for the Yankees, even though they won 497 games and lost 312 for a winning percentage of .614 in that five-year stretch.

Losing the 2001 World Series to the Arizona Diamondbacks—and to have done it with the incomparable Mariano Rivera on the mound—was a bitter disappointment. The Yankees don't suffer disappointments graciously, so in the off-season they went to work in an effort to ensure that such a stain on their record would not recur. Their top priority was to improve an already potent offense, which they achieved by breaking the bank and shelling out $120 million to sign free agent Jason Giambi to a seven-year deal just two years after he had been voted the American League's Most Valuable Player, and by getting together in a rare trade with their crosstown rivals, the Mets, sending outfielder David Justice to Flushing in exchange for Robin Ventura.

The addition of Giambi at first base and the veteran Ventura at third base gave the Yankees two cornerstones to an infield that, with shortstop Derek Jeter's 18 home runs and 75 RBI, and second baseman Alfonso Soriano's 39 homers and 102 RBI, would combine for 125 homers and 392 RBI in the 2002 season. Add to the mix Bernie Williams' 19 homers and 102 RBI, Jorge Posada's 20 homers and 99 RBI, and a pitching staff with 19-game-winner David Wells, 18-game-winner Mike Mussina, 13-game-winners Andy Pettitte and Roger Clemens, backed up by 28 saves from Mariano Rivera. It's no wonder the 2002 Yankees won 103 games, eight more than the previous season, and finished 10½ games ahead of the second-place Boston Red Sox, and why the expectations in the Bronx were that they would return to the top of baseball's heap, and to New York's Canyon of Heroes.

But the Yankees would soon learn that $120 million in 2002 didn't go as far as it once did. After winning Game 1 of the League Division Series, with Rivera rebounding from his Arizona debacle with a scoreless ninth inning for his 25th postseason save in 26 chances, they were blitzed by the wild-card Anaheim Angels in three straight and knocked out of contention for another championship.

It was back to the drawing board—and another major investment—in 2003, with the signing of a three-year, $21 million contract for Hideki Matsui, a 29-year-old superstar from Japan, where his home run prowess earned him the nickname "Godzilla." Humble, proud, hardworking, and thoroughly professional, Matsui played in every game and contributed 16 home runs and 106 runs batted in to a team that won 101 games and its sixth consecutive American League East title.

This time the Yankees breezed through the League Division Series, beating the Minnesota Twins three games to one, with Pettitte, who had led the Yankees with 21 wins during the regular season, winning Game 2, Rivera saving Games 2 and 3, and Jeter batting .429. After that came a heart-palpitating seven-game League Championship Series against the Boston Red Sox. Again, Pettitte won Game 2, Rivera saved Games 3 and 5, and it came down to a sudden death seventh game in Yankee Stadium on Thursday night, October 16.

Down 5–2 in the bottom of the eighth inning to the irrepressible Pedro Martinez, the Yankees were five outs away from another early out in the postseason when, with one out, Jeter, as he has done so often throughout his illustrious career, started a rally with a double which seemed to magically energize his team. Bernie Williams singled to drive in Jeter; Matsui doubled, sending Williams to third; and Posada drove a double to center field that knocked in Williams and Matsui to tie the score at 5–5.

Mariano Rivera took the mound for the ninth inning, gave up a one-out single to Jason Varitek, but retired the next two hitters.

In the 10th, David Ortiz reached Rivera for a double with two outs, but Kevin Millar popped out.

In the 11th, Rivera retired the Sox in order, striking out two. He had pitched two perfect innings against the Twins to save Game 2 of the Division Series, and come back with two more perfect innings and another save in Game 3. Against the Red Sox in the ALCS, he pitched an inning in Game 2, two perfect innings for a save in Game 3, two more innings for a save in Game 5 and now three innings in Game 7. In 15 days Rivera had pitched 12 innings under the most excruciating pressure and allowed just one run, and, with the score still tied 5–5, he said later he was ready to go out for the top of the 12th if there was one.

On the mound for the Red Sox in the bottom of the 11th was the veteran knuckleballer Tim Wakefield, who had come in to pitch the 10th inning in relief and retired the Yankees in order. Leading off for the Yankees was Aaron Boone, a third-generation major leaguer, grandson of two-time All-Star Ray Boone, the younger of two major league sons of four-time All-Star catcher Bob Boone, and brother of three-time All-Star Bret Boone. He had been obtained by the Yankees from the Cincinnati Reds for two minor leaguers and cash just seven weeks earlier. In 54 games with the Yankees covering 189 at-bats, Boone had hit only six home runs, but he would hack at Wakefield's first pitch, a knuckleball, and drive it into the night, deep into the left-field seats, to send the Yankees to the World Series for the 39th time with one of the most dramatic and most memorable home runs in their 101-year history.

So it was on to the World Series against the Florida Marlins, a chance for the Yankees to add to their impressive string of championship trophies.

The Series began on Saturday, October 18, in Yankee Stadium, where Brad Penny out-pitched David Wells to give Florida the first game 3–2.

The Yankees came back in Game 2 and jumped out to a 6–0 lead on Hideki Matsui's three-run homer in the first, an RBI double by Juan Rivera in the second, and Alfonso Soriano's two-run homer in the fourth, all in support of Andy Pettitte, who was making the second game of postseason series his private preserve. Pettitte took his 6–0 lead into the ninth having allowed just four hits, all singles, while walking one and striking out seven.

When the Marlins scored a run in the ninth on two singles sandwiched around an error by Aaron Boone. (How could you fault him? It was because of his game-winning 11th inning home run against the Red Sox a few days earlier that the Yankees were even here.) Pettitte was lifted for Jose Contreras, who got the final out on a ground ball to third. This time Boone handled it and forced the runner at second for the final out to give Pettitte his third win of the 2003 postseason without a defeat.

AARON BOONE

If not for Aaron Boone, Alex Rodriguez might never have been a Yankee.

How's that?

Midway through the 2003 season the Yankees traded third baseman Robin Ventura to the Los Angeles Dodgers and acquired Aaron Boone in a trade with the Cincinnati Reds to be Ventura's replacement. In 54 games, Boone batted .254 with six home runs and 31 RBIs and played a better than adequate third base. But it was in the postseason that Boone became part of Yankees' postseason lore alongside Bucky Dent, Chris Chambliss, Reggie Jackson, Tino Martinez, Scott Brosius, and Jim Leyritz.

Boone's 11th-inning, walk-off home run to win Game 7 of the American League Championship Series over the archrival Boston Red Sox and send the Yankees to the World Series was one of the great dramatic moments in the history of baseball.

It had not been a good series for Boone. In 16 previous at-bats, he had two hits, both singles. But that home run erased all that'd come before. Aaron Boone did not pass Go and he did not collect $200. He went directly into Yankees lore, a hero for the ages.

The story of Aaron Boone's time with the Yankees, however, did not have such a happy ending.

That winter, Boone was playing a pick-up basketball game, a no-no in violation of his major league contract. He cut to free himself from his opponent and felt a pop in his knee. He had torn a ligament. He would need surgery and would be out for the year.

On February 16, the Yankees, in a trade with the Texas Rangers, acquired Alex Rodriguez after he first agreed to move from shortstop to third base.

On March 1, the Yankees released Aaron Boone.

For the middle three games of the Series it was on to sunny Florida, where the Yankees won a 6–1 replica of Game 2, breaking open a tight game with four runs in the ninth on a three-run homer by Bernie Williams and a solo shot by that man Boone to take a two games to one lead.

The Marlins kept their hopes alive by winning the next two games, a 4–3 victory in Game 4 on Alex Gonzalez's home run off Jeff Weaver leading off the bottom of the 12th, and a 6–4 victory in Game 5. Suddenly, the Yankees were down three games to two to this upstart, expansion Marlins team in only the 11th year of its existence. But they were going home for the final two games in Yankee Stadium and they had old reliable Andy Pettitte, who had won his last three postseason decisions, rested and ready for Game 6.

Jack McKeon, the 72-year-old baseball lifer who had taken over during the season from Jeff Torborg as manager of the Marlins, defied custom, tradition, and baseball logic by naming Josh Beckett to pitch Game 6 on three days' rest.

Just as he had been in Game 2, Pettitte was outstanding in Game 6, pitching seven innings, striking out seven, and holding the Marlins to two runs: one on three singles in the fifth, the other an unearned run scored without benefit of a hit in the sixth.

As good as Pettitte was, Beckett, the Marlins' 23-year-old fireballer, was even better. He dominated the Yankee hitters, allowing five hits, walking two, and striking out nine, and stunned the Yankee Stadium crowd with a 2–0 victory.

While they failed to win their 27th World Series, the Yankees at least got there for the sixth time in eight years; and there was always next year.

Or was there?

15   BREAKING UP
THAT OLD GANG

ON DECEMBER 16, 2003, ANDY PETTITTE, TIRED OF BEING AWAY from home, spending too many days away from his wife and three young children, and feeling unwanted by the Yankees, exercised his right to become a free agent and signed a three-year contract worth $31.5 million with his adopted hometown team, the Houston Astros.

Thirty-four days later, Roger Clemens, tired of being away from home, spending too many days away from his wife and four young children, exercised his right to become a free agent and signed a one-year contract worth $5 million with his adopted hometown team, the Houston Astros.

The two events were not considered coincidental.

Back on February 18, 1999, the Yankees had pulled off a huge trade with the Toronto Blue Jays, sending infielder Homer Bush and left-handed pitchers Graeme Lloyd and David Wells north of the border in exchange for future Hall of Fame right-hander Roger Clemens, possessor of 233 major league victories and five Cy Young Awards.

Andy Pettitte was ecstatic. It meant his boyhood idol would be his teammate.

Clemens and Pettitte had much in common. Both were Texans—although Clemens was transplanted from Ohio and Pettitte from Louisiana—both had attended San Jacinto Junior College and both lived in suburban Houston, just minutes away from each other.

In time, Clemens would also become Pettitte's mentor, his role model, his counsel, his pitching guru, and, despite the difference in their ages—Clemens was 36, Pettitte 27—his closest friend, the older brother Andy never had. The two were practically inseparable during the season and in the off-season. They talked pitching constantly. From Clemens, Pettitte learned discipline, pitching strategy, mental toughness, preparedness, competitiveness, and passion.

Their lives and careers were so intertwined it seemed that when one made a move, the other followed.

Between them, Pettitte and Clemens won 38 games for the Yankees in 2003, but still the Yankees could not win the World Series. It was their third straight year without a ride down New York's Canyon of Heroes, and owner George Steinbrenner was not very happy about this sudden turn of events. He demanded action. He wanted changes.

With Pettitte and Clemens both gone, and their 38 wins gone with them, the need to bulk up their pitching staff was the Yankees' first priority and that gave rise to rumors that they were in negotiations with the Arizona Diamondbacks for a trade that would bring the Big Unit, Randy Johnson, to the Bronx. In exchange, Arizona would get a package that included Jorge Posada.

That trade was never consummated, so the Yankees turned their attention elsewhere. They traded three players to acquire pitcher Javier Vazquez from the Montreal Expos, three more to land pitcher Kevin Brown from the Los Angeles Dodgers, and they signed pitchers Jon Lieber and Orlando "El Duque" Hernandez and outfielder Gary Sheffield as free agents.

But their biggest splash of the off-season came on February 16, 2004, when they completed a trade that sent Alfonso Soriano to the Texas Rangers in exchange for superstar Alex Rodriguez, the reigning American League Most Valuable Player, and his $252 million contract, of which there were seven years remaining.

GARY SHEFFIELD

In 22 seasons, three with the Yankees, Gary Sheffield (nephew of Dwight "Doc" Gooden) put up Hall of Fame numbers: a career batting average of .292, 509 home runs, 1,676 RBI, was a nine-time All-Star, and won a National League batting title (.330 with the San Diego Padres in 1992).

Sheffield was a 35-year-old veteran who had played with five other major league teams when the Yankees signed him as a free agent in 2004. He promptly produced two outstanding seasons in the Bronx: a .290 average, 36 homers, and 121 RBI in 2004 and .291, 34, 123 line in 2005. The following year he was off to another great start when on April 29 he injured his wrist in a collision with Shea Hillenbrand of the Toronto Blue Jays. He underwent surgery on the wrist and missed most of the season, playing in only 39 games. After the season, he was traded to Detroit.

A controversial figure throughout his career who has been outspoken, confrontational, and combative, Sheffield will be eligible for the Hall of Fame in 2014. However, despite his statistical qualifications he is not expected to be elected, mainly because he was mentioned in the Mitchell Report as having obtained and used steroids.

Among the new acquisitions, Vazquez, Brown, Lieber, and Hernandez would win 46 games, while Sheffield and Rodriguez (72 home runs and 227 RBI between them) beefed up the offense and enabled the Yankees to win 101 games. Of course, this by no means meant to say that the Yankees didn't miss Clemens and Pettitte, especially in the postseason.

In the Division Series, the Yankees disposed of the Minnesota Twins three games to one before meeting their archrivals the Boston Red Sox in the League Championship Series for the second straight year. The Yankees blistered them in the first three games, 10–7, 3–1, and, what everyone believed was a Red Sox deathblow, a 19–8 modern-day Boston Massacre in front of Red Sox Nation in venerable Fenway Park.

The outcome of the 2004 American League Championship Series seemed a foregone conclusion until the Red Sox began to stir, refusing to roll over and perish.

Faced with an early elimination, ignominiously in their own ballpark, the Red Sox rallied from a 2–0 deficit with three runs in the fifth, but fell behind when the Yankees scored two in the sixth. The Red Sox came to bat in the ninth trailing 4–3 and facing the invincible Mariano Rivera in his second inning of work. Kevin Millar drew a walk to start the bottom of the ninth and Dave Roberts ran for him.

Every baseball player has a weakness. Babe Ruth struck out 1,330 times in his career. Rivera's weakness is holding runners on base, and Roberts exploited that weakness by stealing second in a daring move. He scored on a single to center by Bill Mueller to tie the game at 4–4.

Rivera pitched out of a bases-loaded jam and the game went into extra innings, extending the Red Sox's season, if only temporarily, and delaying the presumably inevitable.

They went to the bottom of the 12th with veteran Paul Quantrill pitching for the Yankees. He gave up a leadoff single to Manny Ramirez and David Ortiz followed with a two-run home run that gave the Red Sox a 6–4 victory, and new life.

They were back in Fenway Park for Game 5 the following

night. This time the Red Sox jumped out in front with two in the first and the Yankees stormed back with a run in the second and three in the sixth to take a 4–2 lead. Again in the eighth, the Red Sox came from behind. Ortiz homered off Tom Gordon to make it a 4–3 game. Millar followed with a walk (déjà vu all over again?) and Roberts ran for him. This time he didn't steal second, but he raced to third when Trot Nixon followed with a single.

The Red Sox had the tying run on third and the lead run on first with no one out, and Joe Torre went to the mound to replace Gordon with Rivera. For the second straight night, Rivera was brought in to pitch in the eighth inning by a manager whose team was ahead in the World Series—three games to none the first night and three games to one the second night. Who was panicking now?

Jason Varitek hit a sacrifice fly and the game was tied 4–4.

In his first 51 postseason games, Rivera had won six, lost none, and saved 24. Now in his last 18 games, he had lost one and blown four saves.

They went to the bottom of the 14th inning, with Esteban Loiaiza pitching for the Yankees. With one out he walked Johnny Damon. With two outs he walked Manny Ramirez. Ortiz followed with a single to center to score Damon with the winning run and the Red Sox had survived another day. But they would have to win two straight games in hostile madhouse Yankee Stadium.

No problem!

In Game 6, pitching with a torn tendon sheath in his foot and a blood-soaked white sock, Curt Schilling went seven courageous and overpowering innings, allowing one run (a seventh-inning home run by Bernie Williams) while striking out four, and the Red Sox evened the Series with a 4–2 victory.

Game 7 was no contest. The Red Sox hit four home runs, two by Johnny Damon, one each by David "Big Papi" Ortiz and Mark Bellhorn, and blew the Yankees away before 56,129 shocked patrons in Yankee Stadium.

Rivera, who did not pitch in Game 6, pitched to one batter in Game 7 and got the Yankees' final out. At the time, the Red Sox were ahead 10–3.

The Red Sox would go on to sweep the St. Louis Cardinals in the World Series and finally conquer "the Curse of the Bambino," so called because after winning five world championships in their first 18 years, the Sox, after selling Babe Ruth to the Yankees, would fail to win another for almost 100 years.

In Houston, Roger Clemens and Andy Pettitte teamed up with staff ace Roy Oswalt to win 130 games over three seasons. Clemens won 18 games and lost four in 2004 for the Astros, who finished second in the National League Central and reached the playoffs as a National League wild-card, where Clemens won one game in the Division Series and one in the League Championship Series.

It's a safe bet that if he was still pitching for the Yankees and in the postseason against the Red Sox, the team that dumped him after the 1996 season (they would not offer him a free agent contract after he had given them 13 years and 192 victories), Clemens would have been motivated enough to stop the bleeding and win one game.

Pettitte won six games and lost four for the Astros in 2004, his season curtailed when he underwent elbow surgery. But he rebounded to win 17 games in 2005 and, no surprise, the Astros made it to the World Series for the first time in their 44-year history. Pettitte won one game in the League Championship Series, but in the World Series Houston was swept in four games by the Chicago White Sox. Pettitte started Game 2, allowed two runs in six innings and left leading 4–2, but the White Sox came back to win it with a run in the bottom of the ninth.

While Pettitte was missing from the Yankees in the 2004–06 seasons, the remaining three members of the Core Four remained intact and thriving.

Mariano Rivera, after his blips in the 2001 and 2004 postseason, saved 130 games in the three-year period, pushing his career total to 413, fourth on the all-time list, ahead of Dennis Eckersley and behind Trevor Hoffman, Lee Smith, and John Franco.

Jorge Posada had a three-year total of 63 homers and 245 RBI giving him 198 home runs (12th on the Yankees' all-time list) and 771 RBI (17th on the Yankees' all-time list).

Derek Jeter batted .292, .309, and .343, had three-year totals of 604 hits, 56 homers, and 245 RBI, and was rapidly moving up on the team's all-time lists with 2,150 hits (seventh) 183 home runs (17th), and 860 RBI (11th).

Without Pettitte in 2005 and 2006, the Yankees finished first in the American League East again, their eighth and ninth consecutive division titles, but both times they failed to advance past the Division Series. In 2005 they were eliminated in five games by the Los Angeles Angels (Mike Mussina, Chien-Ming Wang, and Aaron Small took the losses) and in 2006, they were knocked out in four games by the Detroit Tigers (Mussina, Randy Johnson, and Jaret Wright were losing pitchers).

It cannot be ignored, nor passed off as mere coincidence, that in the three seasons Pettitte was away, the Yankees failed to even reach the World Series. In the nine years Pettitte—the definitive big-game pitcher—was there, the Yankees made it to the World Series six times and won it four times.

Considering his overall postseason record of 18–10 with the Yankees, it is not too great a leap of faith to suggest that had he been there, Pettitte might have changed the outcome of the 2004 ALCS or the Division Series of '05 and '06. Baseball savants were left to wonder if the Yankees might have won one, two, or three more pennants and World Series if Andy Pettitte had never left New York.

16   LIGHTNING (A)ROD

ADDING ALEX RODRIGUEZ (AND GARY SHEFFIELD) TO A LINEUP that already had Bernie Williams, Jason Giambi, Hideki Matsui, Derek Jeter, and Jorge Posada was a coup for the Yankees. Only they could afford to do it, because only they had George Steinbrenner signing the checks. George Steinbrenner liked marquee players and big boppers, liked amassing a roster filled with the game's best players—as many as possible.

Rodriguez was going to make the Yankees unbeatable. But adding him was a mixed blessing for the Yankees. They knew they were getting a superstar player, a huge run producer, an annual Most Valuable Player candidate, and a slugger with a chance to make a run at baseball's all-time career home run record.

They also were getting a player who was a lightning rod for controversy, a player who came with baggage, enormous pride, and an ego to match. He was a shortstop who liked playing there and believed he was the best in the game at the position.

How, people wondered, were ARod and Derek Jeter going to coexist? Like Rodriguez, Jeter had his pride and, even if he didn't flaunt it, an ego about his ability. And like Rodriguez, Jeter was a shortstop who loved playing the position, believed he was pretty good at playing there, and was unwilling to move to another position.

ARod made the grand gesture (some say he was merely posturing) of agreeing to move to third base out of respect for Jeter, whose public persona presented a civility toward Rodriguez. In truth, there was an underlying rivalry, distrust, and envy between them. And then there was The Magazine Article.

Back when he was still a member of the Texas Rangers, in a lengthy piece in *Esquire* magazine, Rodriguez, commenting on the rivalry among major league shortstops, said, "Jeter's been blessed with great talent around him. He's never had to lead. He can just go play and have fun. And he hits second—that's totally different than third and fourth in a lineup. You go into New York, you wanna stop Bernie and O'Neill. You never say, 'Don't let Derek beat you.' He's never your concern."

Jeter heard about or read the article and seethed in silence. He didn't comment, but he didn't forget. There was history between them. They were good friends once, now they were merely teammates—and that meant something to Jeter.

Jeter was the sixth pick in the 1992 MLB amateur draft. The next year, Rodriguez was the No. 1 pick in the draft and he sought out Jeter for advice. They hung out in Florida during the off-season and even had sleepovers at each other's homes. Jeter said that when they first came up to the big leagues, he and Rodriguez talked all the time, especially early in the season because "we both knew if we didn't get off to a good start we might get shipped out."

ARod's comments in the magazine thawed the relationship considerably.

It wasn't the first time that two Yankees stars feuded. Babe Ruth and Lou Gehrig didn't speak for years over some disagreement between their wives. Joe DiMaggio was cool with almost all of his teammates (Lefty Gomez and Billy Martin were two exceptions) and was distant toward Mickey Mantle when the switch-hitter arrived as a rookie in 1951.

The Rodriguez-Jeter feud wasn't even the first one between Yankees that was precipitated by a magazine article. It paralleled the 1977 feud between Reggie Jackson—like Rodriguez the Johnny-come-lately to the Yankees, the new kid on the block, the interloper—and Thurman Munson—like Jeter the incumbent star, team captain, and clubhouse leader.

In a famous *Sport* magazine article, Jackson told the writer, "I'm the straw that stirs the drink. Munson thinks he can be the straw that stirs the drink, but he can only stir it bad."

Rodriguez would learn—just as Jackson did with Munson—that Jeter was the respected, admired, and beloved one to his teammates, and that shortstop was his position and the Yankees were his team and would remain that way until he was ready to walk away.

Jackson would spend the next few years attempting to repair the rift right up until Munson's tragic death in a 1979 airplane crash.

And, like Jackson, Rodriguez has made a concerted effort to mend fences with Jeter.

ARod's immediate reaction once his comments hit the fan was to defend himself by using the shopworn excuse that his words were taken out of context.

"How can I ever dog Derek Jeter?" he said. "It's impossible. There is nothing to knock. He's a great defensive player. He's a great offensive player. He's one of the top three players in the game, for the greatest team of my era.

"It's my mistake because I said it. It's not the journalist's fault. It's been my fault for just talking the game and being too general. I guess you have to be very specific. When you say you don't go into New York trying to stop Derek, to me that's more of a team compliment. When you come to Texas now, you don't say you have to stop Ivan [Rodriguez], Alex or Raffy [Rafael Palmeiro]. You say 'Let's stop one through nine because everybody can hurt you."

It wasn't ARod's only mistake where Jeter was concerned. Soon after he signed his record $252 million, 10-year contract, he said the salary was going to be difficult to top, even for Jeter.

"It's going to be hard for him to break that," Rodriguez said, "because he just doesn't do the power numbers and defensively he doesn't do all those things."

While Jeter remained mute on the subject of the feud, his Yankees teammates and friends came to his defense, pointing out that before ARod arrived in the Bronx, in the previous 10 years the Yankees with Jeter won six American League pennants and four World Series. Over the same 10 years, the Seattle Mariners and Texas Rangers with Alex Rodriguez won none.

When reports of the coolness between Jeter and Rodriguez surfaced the fans naturally took sides. Not surprisingly, they lined up with Jeter and greeted ARod with boos. It was suggested that Jeter could put an end to the "Bronx cheers" by publicly expressing his support for his teammate. To that idea, ARod said thanks, but no thanks.

"I'm a big boy," he said. "I should be able to handle myself out there."

Eventually, maturity set in and time began to heal old wounds. Although there would no longer be sleepovers between them, ARod and Jeter settled into an uneasy truce. While the media continued to report that bad blood still existed between the two Yankees, ARod said his attempt to make it appear that his friendship with Jeter remained strong was something of a sham. For years he pretended he and Jeter were still as close as ever—which they weren't—and maintained they were great friends—which they weren't—and that "Things couldn't be better"—which they could. The truth of his relationship with Jeter, said Rodriguez, was neither warm and fuzzy nor icy cold, but somewhere in between.

"People start assuming that things are a lot worse than what they are, which they're not," Rodriguez told a group of writers.

"But they're obviously not as great as they used to be. We were like blood brothers. You don't have to go to dinner with a guy four, five times a week to do what you're doing. It's actually much better than all you guys expect, but I just want the truth to be known

"So let's make a contract. You don't ask me about Derek anymore and I promise to stop lying to all you guys."

Again, Jeter had no comment, but, probably for the good of the team, he could be seen engaging Rodriguez in small talk around the batting cage, in the dugout and in the clubhouse. And when ARod hit his 600th career home run against Toronto on August 4, 2010, Jeter was the first one to greet him at home plate.

The previous night, Rodriguez was 0-for-3 in a loss to the Blue Jays, extending his hitless streak to 17 at-bats and his homerless streak to 46 at-bats. Jeter took the occasion to approach Rodriguez in the clubhouse after the game and sit down with him for a pep talk.

"Just try to get a base hit," the Captain suggested. "Maybe even bunt."

The next day Jeter opened the bottom of the first with a single through the left side. After Nick Swisher and Mark Teixeira were retired, Rodriguez drove a tremendous shot over the center-field fence for career home run No. 600, scoring Jeter ahead of him. (Coincidentally, exactly three years to the day earlier, ARod hit his 500th career home run also with Jeter on base.)

Waiting at home plate for Rodriguez to arrive, Jeter greeted him with a warm embrace and a smile.

"Well," said Jeter, "there goes the bunting situation."

Later, Jeter said, "I'm happy that we on the team were able to watch him achieve it. And I'm happy that he had a chance to do it at home. It's a special moment. It's well deserved."

17   RETURN OF
THE PRODIGAL

THREE SEASONS WITH THE HOUSTON ASTROS APPARENTLY CON-
vinced Andy Pettitte that home cooking just isn't what it's cracked up
to be. Those three seasons also drove home to Pettitte how much he
missed New York, the Yankees, his old teammates, and pitching in
the World Series. So, on December 8, 2006, once more a free agent,
Pettitte signed a one-year, $16 million contract with the Yankees.

It took Roger Clemens only five months to follow his best
friend back to the Yankees.

While Pettitte and Clemens were being welcomed back like
conquering heroes, their return was viewed by many as too late
to reverse the decline of the so-called "Evil Empire," the tag put
on the Yankees by Boston Red Sox chief executive officer Larry
Lucchino. It also was believed to be too late to save Torre, who
was being accused in some quarters of losing his grip on the situation having failed to advance past the Division Series in each of
the two previous playoffs.

Torre faced a crisis in Game 4 of the 2006 Division Series against
the Detroit Tigers. After winning the first game of the series 8–4,

the Yanks dropped the next two games 4–3 and 6–0, and were one defeat away from their second straight KO in the first round of the playoffs. In an effort to right the ship, Torre identified Alex Rodriguez as the chief culprit in his team's demise. In the first three games, ARod had been held to one hit in 11 at-bats (four strikeouts and nine runners left on base), and hadn't driven in a run in 11 straight playoff games, dating back to 2004.

As a result, for Game 4, Torre dropped Rodriguez from fourth to eighth in the batting order, a move that the proud and ego-driven Rodriguez viewed as an insult. He hadn't batted that low in a lineup since May 7, 1996, when he was a 20-year-old shortstop for the Seattle Mariners.

"It was very disappointing to see my name there," Rodriguez said. "Yes, I was embarrassed. But it's not my job to judge or even have an opinion on it. I've got to look at myself in the mirror and say, 'What the hell did I do to get in that situation?' I never questioned Joe. So it's always about me."

ARod held his tongue and spent time with Reggie Jackson, who suffered his own indignity from Billy Martin when he was benched in the final game of the 1977 American League Championship Series against the Kansas City Royals. Jackson sat, but got his chance in the eighth inning. With the Yankees trailing 3–1, he pinch-hit and singled in the Yanks' second run. They would score three more in the ninth to advance to the World Series.

Nine days later, in one of the greatest displays in World Series history, Jackson hit three home runs on three pitches against the Los Angeles Dodgers to clinch the Yankees 21st world championship and earn the nickname "Mr. October."

Now, 29 years after his greatest performance, Jackson was imparting the wisdom of his own experience on Rodriguez.

"I told him not to worry about it, go in there and play. He's happy he's in the lineup and he's got a chance to help."

Batting Rodriguez eighth in Game 4 of the 2006 Division Series against the Tigers proved to be no panacea for Torre and the Yankees. ARod continued in his funk, going hitless in three at-bats to finish the series 1-for-14, a batting average of .071 with no RBI and four strikeouts, and the Yankees lost 8–3 and slipped quietly into the off-season.

Proving you actually can go home again, Pettitte stepped right in and won 15 games in 2007, second on the team to Chien-Ming Wang, a right-hander from Taiwan who won 19 games for the Yankees for the second straight season.

Despite the 34 wins from their two top pitchers, Pettitte and Wang; Rivera's 30 saves; Jeter's .322 average, 12 homers, and 73 RBI; Posada's .338 average, 20 homers, and 90 RBI; a monster MVP season from a rejuvenated Alex Rodriguez of .314/54/156; a combined 60 homers and 301 RBI from Hideki Matsui, Bobby Abreu, and the youngster Robinson Cano; and 94 wins, the Yankees came in second in the AL East, two games behind the Red Sox.

Finishing second to the Red Sox didn't sit well with the Boss, George Steinbrenner. There was unrest in the Bronx. To add to Torre's plight, as the American League wild-card, the Yankees' first-round playoff opponent would be the Cleveland Indians. It was in Cleveland where Steinbrenner made his reputation and his fortune as president of the American Ship Building Company. He was raised in a Cleveland suburb and had investments and many friends still in Cleveland. Losing to the Indians was unacceptable and would not be tolerated.

Nevertheless, the Yankees proved to be no match for the Indians, who beat the Yankees in the best-of-five series, three games to one. Not even the return of Andy Pettitte could save the Yankees.

In Game 1, the Indians pounded 14 hits off of four Yankees pitchers in a 12–4 rout and, once again, Torre turned to Pettitte in Game 2. Andy was on his game. He was better than that. He was brilliant, holding the Indians scoreless and departing with a 1–0 lead with one out in the seventh inning. But the Indians tied the game in the eighth on a wild pitch by Joba Chamberlain, who lost his composure on the mound when he was attacked by a swarm of bugs called midges.

The Indians went on to win 2–1 in 11 innings to go up two games to none, and both manager Joe Torre and catcher Jorge Posada were taken to task in the press by their failure to come to the aid of their beleaguered reliever.

The press maintained that either the manager or the catcher should have gone to the mound to calm the young pitcher or called time, but neither did a thing.

The Yankees returned home needing a sweep of the next three games to advance to the League Championship Series. There was hope when the Yankees won Game 3 by a score of 8–4. Now they needed to win one more game in order to send Pettitte out for a climactic Game 5. But Andy never got another chance, as the Indians scored two runs in the first and two more in the second off Wang, knocked him out, and handed him his second defeat of the series, 6–4. The Yankees were done and so, as it turned out, was Torre.

To add to Posada's frustration and embarrassment, he made the final out of the Series.

ROBINSON CANO

In eight seasons, Robinson Cano has gone from being a top prospect in the minors to a superstar of major league baseball, a worthy successor to the Yankees' line of superstars that extends from Ruth to Gehrig to DiMaggio to Mantle to Jeter. Cano has hit at least 14 home runs in each of his eight seasons, has averaged 89 runs batted in a season, and has a career batting average of .308.

Cano was born in San Pedro de Macoris, the Dominican Republic, but his family spent three years in the United States and Robinson attended Newark, New Jersey, schools in the seventh, eighth, and ninth grades before the family returned to the Dominican Republic. Robinson's father, Jose, appeared in six games as a pitcher for the Houston Astros in 1989. Jose Cano named his son Robinson in honor of Jackie Robinson, and as homage to his namesake Cano wears Yankees uniform No. 24, Jackie Robinson's No. 42 in reverse.

When Cano won the Home Run Derby during the 2011 All-Star Game festivities he conjured up thoughts of a scene from *Field of Dreams* by choosing his dad to be his batting practice pitcher.

When the season ended, Posada officially became a free agent with a chance to make a big score that would set him up financially for life. The Yankees' crosstown rivals, the New York Mets, came at Posada hard, offering him a five-year contract. But Posada, preferring to finish his career with the only team he had ever played for, turned down the Mets' offer and agreed with the Yankees on a four-year contract for $52 million.

Against the Indians in the Division Series, Jeter batted .176 with one RBI. Posada hit .133 and didn't drive in a run. Rivera appeared in three games, pitched 4⅔ scoreless innings, allowed two hits, and struck out six, but never was in a position to win or save a game.

The Yankees and Torre were done. In 12 years he had won 10 division titles, six pennants, and four World Series championships, but it had been seven years since they had won their last one, and that was unacceptable.

In failing health, George Steinbrenner no longer was ruling the Yankees' roost as "the Boss." He had turned control of the team over to his sons, Hank and Hal (the latter as managing general partner), and to team president Randy Levine and senior vice president/general manager Brian Cashman.

Within the Yankees front office there were pro-Torre and anti-Torre factions—those that wanted him replaced and those that thought he deserved to remain in control. There were also many who feared the public backlash if the Yankees dumped the popular Torre, whose fate would be discussed at a meeting in Steinbrenner's Tampa home.

It was decided by the group to offer Torre a one-year contract for $5 million with performance incentives that could bring the total amount to $8 million. Torre would still be the highest-paid manager in baseball, but the cut in salary was a drastic and insulting one. He insisted that he didn't deserve a cut in pay, but the Yankees remained adamant and severed relations with their manager.

For Torre's replacement, the Yankees selected Joe Girardi, who was the Yankees' catcher from 1996 to 1999, after which he spent three seasons with the Chicago Cubs and one with the St. Louis Cardinals. When he retired as a player, Girardi returned to the Yankees as a television analyst. Later, he joined Torre's staff as bench coach and catching instructor. In 2006, he was named manager of the Florida Marlins, with whom he finished in fourth place in the National League East and was named NL Manager of the Year.

A disagreement with ownership caused Girardi to resign as manager of the Marlins after only one season, and he returned to the Yankees broadcast booth for a year until he was named Torre's successor on a three-year contract.

18   MOVING DAY

THE 2008 SEASON WAS THE BEGINNING OF ONE ERA AND THE end of another in the long and glorious history of the New York Yankees. Next year there would be a magnificent, majestic, brand-new Yankee Stadium rising out of the rubble next to the famed "House That Ruth Built" that Col. Jacob Ruppert had conceived 85 years earlier. For now there was a new manager calling the shots and making the moves on the field.

The Joe Girardi era got off to a shaky start, struggling on a win-one-lose-one diet in its early days. On May 20, after losing three out of four to Tampa Bay (George Steinbrenner's adopted home), two games to the hated Mets, and one to the Orioles, the Yankees were 20–25 and had fallen into last place in the American League East, 7½ games out of first.

Had Boss Steinbrenner still been calling the shots, he might have done what he did several times in the past and fired his manager right then, and there never would have been a Joe Girardi Year Two. But it was not the old reckless, impatient, impetuous, impulsive, hair-trigger Boss in charge, it was a younger, more patient, more fiscally prudent Steinbrenner, his son Hal, making these decisions now, and he was willing to give Girardi a little more rope.

From June 12 to June 19, the Yanks won seven straight games, moved over the .500 mark to 40–33, and climbed out of the cellar into third place, five games out of first. It was as high as they would get all season and their lowest finish in 16 years.

The final game at the "old" Yankee Stadium came on Sunday night, September 21, against the Baltimore Orioles, a lovely late-summer evening that was perfect for baseball and for nostalgia as 54,610 fans crammed into the old ballpark, swelling the season's attendance to an all-time Yankees record of 4,298,655.

The pregame ceremonies were a testimony to Yankees past and present, living and dead. Former Yankees, as many as could be contacted, were brought back to Yankee Stadium. They were introduced to the crowd and they ran, trotted, or walked out to the position they had occupied in their playing days. Later, those players were joined at their positions by widows, children, and grandchildren of those players who had played those positions and had passed on.

Among active players, special acknowledgment was accorded the Core Four, the oldest Yankees in point of service.

Jorge Posada, who would miss the last 65 games of the season after undergoing arthroscopic shoulder surgery in July, and batted .268 with three home runs and 22 RBI in 51 games, was asked to receive the pregame first ball thrown out by Babe Ruth's 91-year-old daughter, Julia Ruth Stevens.

Andy Pettitte had the honor of starting the last game at the stadium. He pitched five innings, recorded the 2,000[th] strikeout of his career in the second inning, and earned the victory, evening his season's record at 14–14.

Mariano Rivera, who would finish the season with 39 saves and 482 for his career, came into the game to the strains of "Enter Sandman" for the final time in the old Stadium. He pitched the ninth inning in a non-save situation and retired the Orioles in order on three ground balls.

Derek Jeter, who would bat an even .300 for the season with 11 home runs and 69 runs batted in, would be removed from the game with two outs in the top of the ninth so he might hear, one more time, the crowd, led by the Bleacher Creatures, chant, "DER-ek JEE-ter" as he jogged off the field. He ducked into the dugout and then popped his head out for a brief curtain call.

Later, it would be Jeter's duty as captain to represent the current Yankees team in addressing the capacity crowd. Speaking without notes ("I just sort of winged it," he would say), his remarks were clear, concise, heartfelt, and eloquently simple:

"For all of us out here, it's a huge honor to put this uniform on every day and come out here and play. And every member of this organization, past and present, has been calling this place home for 85 years. It's a lot of tradition, a lot of history, and a lot of memories. The great thing about memories is you're able to pass them along from generation to generation. And although things are going to change next year and we're going to move across the street, there are a few things with the New York Yankees that never change. That's pride, tradition, and most of all, we have the greatest fans in the world. We're relying on you to take the memories from this stadium, add them to the memories that come in the new Yankee Stadium, and continue to pass them on from generation to generation.

"So, on behalf of the entire organization we just want to take this moment to salute you, the greatest fans in the world."

With those words, Jeter removed his cap to salute the crowd while behind him his teammates did the same.

The Yankees played the final six games of the 2008 season in Toronto and Boston, ending up with a record of 89–73 (five fewer wins than Joe Torre's last Yankees team the previous season and their fewest wins in eight years). They finished in third place, eight games out, behind the Tampa Bay Rays and the Boston Red Sox, and were left out of the postseason for the first time in 14 years.

While Derek Jeter batted an even .300 (the 10th time in his career he had reached the precious .300 mark), his critics pointed out that it was his lowest season's average in four years, his 69 RBI and 11 home runs were five-year lows, and he was crowding his 35th birthday. Some even said that on defense Jeter had lost a step (or two) and suggested that the Yankees would be best served moving him off shortstop to center field, which Robin Yount had done a decade earlier on his way to the Hall of Fame.

Jeter bristled at the notion and vowed to work hard during the off-season on a conditioning program that would improve his speed and quickness. With a new home and a new beginning, he was determined to put up the kind of numbers that would cause his critics to choke on their words.

19 CORE FOURS
OF THE PAST

AS YANKEE STADIUM CLOSED FOR GOOD, YANKEES FANS AND HIS-torians found themselves looking back at the fascinating legacy the team had left behind. Mariano Rivera, Andy Pettitte, Jorge Posada, and Derek Jeter did not comprise the only "Core Four" of Yankees' legend, merely the most successful and the one that remained together for the longest period.

The Yankees won at least one World Series in six consecutive decades from the 1920s through the 1970s. Presented herewith are the Core Four representing each decade, chosen not only for their singular performance on the playing field but also for their longevity as a unit.

THE '20s

Babe Ruth, Bob Meusel, Lou Gehrig, Waite Hoyt
Years as Yankees Teammates—7 (1923-29)
Pennants Won as Teammates—4
World Series Won as Teammates—3

The Yankees had not won a thing in their 17-year history as both Yankees and Highlanders until Babe Ruth was purchased from the Boston Red Sox on January 3, 1920. That season they would improve from 80 victories to 95, yet finish third in the eight-team American League. But over the next 12 seasons, Ruth would lead them to seven pennants and four world championships, including the amazing 1927 season when Ruth belted a record 60 home runs while leading the famed "Murderers' Row" to a World Series victory. That year the Yankees had a record of 110–44, for a winning percentage of .714, the exact number of home runs hit by Ruth in his career.

Bob Meusel was an ornery, mean, cranky outfielder whose career as a Yankee covered the entire decade of the 1920s. Born in San Jose, California, on July 19, 1896, he was purchased from Vernon in the Pacific Coast League, arrived with the Yankees in 1920, alternated with Babe Ruth between left field and right field, and left after the 1929 season. He played one season with Cincinnati before retiring from major league baseball. The younger brother of National League star Irish Meusel, Bob ranks eighth on the Yankees all-time list in batting average at .311 and 12th in RBI with 1,013. In 1925, when Ruth missed 50 games with his famous "bellyache," Meusel led the American League in home runs with 33 and RBI with 138.

New York native Lou Gehrig, the "Iron Horse," was discovered by the Yankees while playing baseball at Columbia University and signed by legendary Yankees scout Paul Krichell. He joined the Yankees in 1923 and got his big break two years later when first baseman Wally Pipp asked out of the lineup because of a headache. Gehrig stepped in and played in 2,130 consecutive games, a major league record that stood until 1995, when it was broken by the Baltimore Orioles' Cal Ripken Jr. Gehrig ended his streak voluntarily when he removed himself from the starting lineup before a game in Detroit on May 2, 1939. On June 21, the Yankees announced that Gehrig's uniform No. 4 would be permanently retired. On July 4, between games of a doubleheader at Yankee Stadium, the Yankees staged "Lou Gehrig Appreciation Day" at which Gehrig, in a poignant speech, proclaimed, "Today, I consider myself the luckiest man on the face of the earth." Just under two years later Gehrig passed away from amyotrophic lateral sclerosis, better known as Lou Gehrig's Disease.

Waite Hoyt was another local boy, born in Brooklyn and educated at Erasmus Hall High School, which was also attended by football's Al Davis and Sid Luckman; basketball's Ned Irish and Billy Cunningham; Olympic swimmer Eleanor Holm; chess champion Bobby Fischer; actresses Mae West, Barbara Stanwyck, and Susan Hayward; opera star Beverly Sills; pop singers Barbra Streisand and Neil Diamond; and author Mickey Spillane. On December 15, 1920, Hoyt was acquired by the Yankees from the Boston Red Sox. He would twice win 20 games among his 157 wins as a Yankee (all but two in the decade of the '20s), ninth on their all-time list. Hoyt was elected to the Hall of Fame in 1969 by the Veterans Committee.

THE '30s

Lou Gehrig, Tony Lazzeri, Bill Dickey, Red Ruffing
Years as Yankees Teammates—8 (1930–37)
Pennants Won as Teammates—3
World Series Won as Teammates—3

With Babe Ruth in decline, Lou Gehrig took over as the Yankees' go-to guy in the '30s. In the decade he would lead the league in home runs and runs batted in three times each, win one batting title, hit 40 or more home runs four times, get 200 or more hits six times, and drive in 100 or more runs nine straight years until his retirement in 1939.

Tony "Poosh 'Em Up" Lazzeri is one of several Yankees born in the San Francisco Bay Area (Joe DiMaggio, Frank Crosetti, Lefty Gomez, Ping Bodie, Jerry Coleman, and Billy Martin were as well). In 1925, he hit 60 home runs for Salt Lake City in the Pacific Coast League and was sold to the New York Yankees after the season. In 12 seasons with the Yankees he hit 169 home runs, including 18 in 1927, which was third in the American League behind his Yankees teammates, Babe Ruth (60) and Lou Gehrig (47). Seven times in his career—four of them in the '30s—Lazzeri drove in more than 100 runs. He is one of only 14 players in major league history to hit a "natural" cycle. On June 3, 1932, in a 20–13 romp over the Athletics in Philadelphia's Shibe Park, Lazzeri struck, in order, a single, double, triple, and home run (which just happened to be a grand slam). On May 24, 1936, again in Shibe Park against the Athletics, in a 25–2 slaughter, he became the first player in MLB history to hit two grand slams in a game while setting a record with 11 RBI.

William Malcolm "Bill" Dickey of Bastrop, Louisiana, spent his entire 17-year career with the Yankees and finished with a career .313 batting average (seventh on their all-time list), 202 home runs (15th), and 1,209 RBI (8th). He showed his durability when he set a major league record by catching 100 games or more for 13 consecutive seasons. In the decade of the 1930s, Dickey had four straight seasons with at least 20 home runs and 100 RBI, and nine seasons with a batting average of .300 or better. In 1946, after Joe McCarthy abruptly resigned as manager of the Yankees, Dickey took over as player/manager for 105 games. He retired after the 1946 season, but returned in 1949 as a coach whose job was to help school Yogi Berra to continue the line of succession as Yankees catcher. As Berra would say, "Bill Dickey taught me all his experiences."

Charles Herbert "Red" Ruffing was traded by the Red Sox to the Yankees on May 6, 1930, and spent the next 15 seasons as the ace of the Yanks' pitching staff, winning 231 games (second on their all-time list), striking out 1,526 batters (fourth), pitching 261 complete games (first), and 40 shutouts (tied for second with Mel Stottlemyre). He won at least 20 games for four consecutive seasons (1936–39). Ruffing also was one of the best hitting pitchers in baseball history, with a lifetime batting average of .269 and 273 runs batted in for 22 seasons with the Yankees, Red Sox, and White Sox. He is fourth on the all-time list of home runs by a pitcher with 34 (he also hit two as a pinch hitter).

THE '40s

Joe DiMaggio, Charlie Keller, Tommy Henrich, Phil Rizzuto
Years as Yankees Teammates—6 (1941–42, 1946–49)
Pennants Won as Teammates—4
World Series Won as Teammates—3

With Lou Gehrig gone, the baton passed to Joe DiMaggio as the leader of the Yankees. After the 1934 season, DiMaggio, the middle of three major league–playing brothers (with Vince and Dom), was acquired from the San Francisco Seals of the Pacific Coast League, where he'd hit safely in 61 consecutive games in 1933. The Yankees paid $25,000 for DiMaggio, plus five players and a promise to allow Joe to remain with the Seals for the 1935 season, in which he batted .398, hit 34 homers, drove in 154 runs, and was named PCL Most Valuable Player. In 1936, his first season with the Yankees, DiMaggio amassed one of the greatest rookie seasons in major league history: a .323 average, 206 hits, 44 doubles, a league-leading 15 triples, 29 home runs, and 125 RBI. Over the next five seasons he would bat .346, .324, .381, .352, and .357, hit 169 home runs, and drive in 691 runs. In 1941, he hit safely in a still-standing major league–record 56 consecutive games and, perhaps most remarkably, in 622 plate appearances he struck out only 13 times. DiMaggio finished his career with a lifetime batting average of .325, 361 homers, 1,537 RBI, and only 369 strikeouts. He might have compiled even more impressive numbers, but his career was held to only 13 seasons by a series of leg and foot injuries and by having lost three of his prime years—1943 to 1945—to military service during World War II.

Because of his strength, they called Charlie Keller "King Kong," but never to his face. He hated the nickname and would never answer to it. Keller was a bear of a man and a hard-nosed, powerful slugger who served as protection for Joe DiMaggio in the Yankees' lineup. Keller became the first rookie ever to hit two home runs in a World Series game when he did it against Cincinnati in Game 3 of the 1939 Series. Three times Keller hit at least 30 home runs in a season and three times he knocked in at least 100 runs. When he retired from baseball, Keller founded Yankeeland Farm in Maryland and had an enormously successful career as a breeder of harness horses.

On April 14, 1937, the Cleveland Indians were forced by Major League Baseball to release a young minor league outfielder named Tommy Henrich. Five days later, the Yankees signed him, and 22 days after that Henrich made his major league debut in the start of what would be a remarkable 11-year major league career (including three years out for military service) all with the Yankees. Teaming with center fielder Joe DiMaggio and left fielder Charlie Keller, Henrich in right field helped form one of the best hitting outfields of his era. Henrich had a career batting average of .282 with 183 home runs and 795 RBI, but it was his distinguished work in four World Series which helped earn him the nickname "Old Reliable." In Game 1 of the 1949 World Series, Henrich hit the first "walk-off" home run in Series history when he drove a 2–0 pitch from Don Newcombe into the right-field seats at Yankee Stadium to give the Yanks a 1–0 victory over the Brooklyn Dodgers. Henrich was in the center of one of the most memorable moments in World

Series history in Game 4 of the 1941 World Series. The Yankees were leading the Brooklyn Dodgers two games to one, but the Dodgers were ahead in Game 3 by a score of 4–3 with two outs, nobody on base, and Henrich up to bat in the top of the ninth. Henrich swung and missed a 3–2 pitch from Hugh Casey. But when catcher Mickey Owen let the ball get by him for a passed ball, Henrich reached first base. The Yankees then rallied for four runs to win the game 7–4, and went on to take the Series four games to one.

Told by the New York Giants and Brooklyn Dodgers that at 5'6" and 150 pounds he was too small, Brooklyn-born Phil "Scooter" Rizzuto signed with the New York Yankees and went on to be chosen American League Most Valuable Player in 1950, be elected to the Hall of Fame, and to spend more than a half-century with the Yankees as a player and beloved broadcaster. In 13 seasons as an All-Star shortstop, Rizzuto, acclaimed as one of the great bunters in baseball history, batted .273, accumulated 1,588 hits, played outstanding defense, and helped the Yankees win nine pennants and seven World Series. Ted Williams once said that if his Red Sox had Rizzuto as their shortstop, the Sox, not the Yankees, would have won all those championships. As a broadcaster, Rizzuto was known for his malaprops, sending birthday wishes to fans, friends, and restaurateurs, and his signature comments, "You huckleberry" and "Holy Cow." Someone once looked at Rizzuto's score card and noticed the entry WW. Asked what sort of play was WW, Rizzuto replied, "Wasn't watching."

THE '50s

Mickey Mantle, Whitey Ford, Yogi Berra, Hank Bauer
Years as Yankees Teammates—7 (1953–1959)
Pennants Won as Teammates—5
World Series Won as Teammates—3

The line of Yankees superstars continued in 1951 with the arrival of switch-hitting Mickey Mantle, one of the greatest, strongest, most popular and revered players in baseball history. Known for his prodigious home runs, his shot on April 17, 1953, off Chuck Stobbs of the Washington Senators in Griffith Stadium was said to have traveled 565 feet and introduced into the baseball lexicon the phrase "tape-measure home run." On May 22, 1963, he hit a ball that almost became the first ever to sail out of Yankee Stadium, and on September 10, 1960, he hit one over the roof at Tiger Stadium that was calculated to have traveled 643 feet. In his 18-year career, all with the Yankees, Mantle batted .298, hit 536 home runs, drove in 1,509 runs, and won three Most Valuable Player Awards. Twice in his career he hit 50 home runs or more, four times he hit 40 or more, and nine times he hit 30 or more. In 1956, he won the Triple Crown with a .353 average, 52 home runs, and 130 RBI. As staggering as his numbers are, they might have been even greater had he not suffered with a variety of injuries that caused him to play fewer than 130 games six times in his 18 seasons.

Elston Howard, his longtime battery mate, dubbed him "the Chairman of the Board." Whitey Ford, another New York native who starred for and played his entire career with his hometown team, is all over the Yankees all-time leader board for pitchers: first in wins (236), strikeouts (1,956), games started (438), innings (3,170), and shutouts (45), third in winning percentage (.690), and tied for sixth in complete games (156). Ford came up to the Yankees midway through the 1950 season and made his major league debut on July 1. He helped the Yankees win the American League pennant by winning nine of his 10 decisions and then was the winning pitcher in the clinching game of the World Series against the Philadelphia Phillies. Ford spent the next two seasons in military service, returning to the Yankees in 1953 to begin a stretch of 13 consecutive seasons with double figures in wins, including 25 in 1961 and 24 in 1963. In 1961, Ford broke the record of 29⅔ consecutive scoreless innings in the World Series, held by Babe Ruth (set in 1918 when he pitched for the Boston Red Sox), ultimately raising the record to 33⅔ innings.

Nobody doesn't like Sara Lee...or Yogi Berra. We don't know if Sara could hit a curveball, but we know that Berra could, and did. One of the most beloved baseball players ever to play the game, Berra has a .285 lifetime average, 358 home runs, and 1,430 RBI in 2,120 major league games as proof. Berra arrived with the Yankees fresh out of the U.S. Navy to appear in seven games in 1946. He would stay for 18 seasons as a player, during which he was one of only four players in baseball history to win three Most Valuable Player Awards (1951, 1954, 1955). A notorious "bad ball" hitter who would connect with balls that hit the dirt or were over his head, Berra's greatest attribute was having played on 14 pennant winners and 10 World Series winners in his 18 years as a Yankee. Casey Stengel, who managed the Yankees from 1949 to 1960, called Berra "my assistant manager." After retiring in 1963, Berra served nine years in two tenures as a Yankees coach and three more—also in two tenures—as the Yankees manager. He also managed the New York Mets and is one of only seven managers to win pennants in each league. The Yogi Berra Museum on the campus of Montclair State University in New Jersey is a shrine to Berra's career, including displays of his memorabilia and his famous malaprops, or "Berraisms," such as, "Nobody goes there anymore, it's too crowded," "You can observe a lot by watching," "I want to thank all those who made this night necessary," and "It ain't over 'til it's over."

Hank Bauer was a rugged, rough and tumble ex-Marine who someone once said, "has a face like a clenched fist." The comment, Bauer's looks, his gravelly voice, and his reputation belie the docile nature of a gentle soul. But on the playing field, he was hardly that. A tough, hell-for-leather, win-at-all-costs, fierce competitor, he would often confront lackadaisical rookies with the

admonition, "You're messing with my money." A four-year veteran of the Marines and a war hero who won 11 campaign ribbons,
including two Bronze Stars and two Purple Hearts in the Pacific
Theater during World War II, Bauer was signed by the Yankees
in 1946. Two years later he reached the major leagues. Like Yogi
Berra and other Yankees of that era, Bauer was all about winning.
In his 12 seasons with them, the Yankees won nine pennants and
seven World Series. He set a record by hitting safely in 17 consecutive World Series games. When his playing career ended, Bauer
managed the Athletics in both Kansas City and Oakland, and the
Baltimore Orioles, with whom he won the 1966 World Series in a
four-game sweep of the Los Angeles Dodgers.

THE '60s

Mickey Mantle, Roger Maris, Elston Howard, Bobby Richardson
Years as Yankees Teammates—7 (1960-66)
Pennants Won as Teammates—5
World Series Won as Teammates—3

By the 1960s, Mickey Mantle, having reached veteran, exalted,
legendary status, was the leader of the Yankees not only on the
field, but in the clubhouse as well. He was adored by fans, respected by opponents, and revered by teammates. While his age
and the frequency of his physical ailments indicated that he would
soon begin his decline, there were still some good years remaining
for Mantle. In 1960, he led the league with 40 home runs. In 1961,
he made a bid to break Babe Ruth's record of 60 homers, ending
up with 54 and 128 RBI. Injuries reduced him over the next two
seasons to a combined 188 games, 45 homers, and 124 RBI, numbers he used to ring up in a 154-game season. He rebounded with
35 homers and 111 RBI in 1964, but again injuries hampered him
in 1965 and '66, when he hit 42 homers and drove in 102 runs in

Derek Jeter raises a fist to the sky after hitting a game-winning homer in the bottom of the 10th inning off of Byung-Hyun Kim in Game 4 of the 2001 World Series against the Arizona Diamondbacks.

In 2003, the Core Four made their sixth trip to the Fall Classic (the 39th time the Yankees appeared in the World Series), but lost to the Florida Marlins. Pettitte would leave the following year for Houston.

By 2007, the Core Four were back together. Here Mariano Rivera, Andy Pettitte, Derek Jeter, and Jorge Posada prepare to address the media during 2009 spring training. *(AP Images)*

The Yankees and their fans celebrate as Mariano Rivera hugs Jeter following Jeter's 2,772nd hit, which passed Lou Gehrig for the most ever by a Yankee.

Mariano Rivera looks on smiling as manager Joe Girardi presents Rivera's youngest son, Jaziel, with a gift in honor of Mariano's 500th career save. *(AP Images)*

Jorge Posada, Andy Pettitte, Derek Jeter, and Mariano Rivera celebrate with the Commissioner's Trophy after winning the 2009 World Series over the Philadelphia Phillies.

Derek Jeter is mobbed by Yankees (including Mariano Rivera and Jorge Posada) upon collecting his 3,000th career hit, a home run against the Tampa Bay Rays at Yankee Stadium on Saturday, July 9, 2011. *(AP Images)*

At Jorge Posada's retirement press conference on January 24, 2012; he is flanked by fellow members of the Core Four, Mariano Rivera and Derek Jeter. The three stand before the five World Series trophies they won as Yankee teammates. *(AP Images)*

Following Posada's retirement and Rivera's season-ending knee injury, it fell to the 38-year-old Jeter and the 40-year-old Pettitte to drive the Yankees to the postseason once more. They finished the 2012 season with the best record in the AL.

230 games. It was clear the end was in sight. He played the 1967–68 seasons as a shell of his former self, 144 games each season with un-Mantle-like batting averages of .245 and .237, 22 and 18 home runs, and 55 and 54 RBI. He could have played another year for the same $100,000 salary, but his pride wouldn't allow it and he retired to Yankees superstar emeritus status.

The Yankees targeted Roger Maris when he came up with the Cleveland Indians as a 22-year-old and hit 42 home runs in his first two seasons. They liked his left-handed stroke and saw him as a dead-pull hitter capable of doing severe damage in Yankee Stadium's short right-field porch. Unable to pry him away from Indians general manager Frank Lane, the Yanks waited two years, when Maris was with their frequent trading partner the Kansas City Athletics, and landed him on December 11, 1959, in a seven-player trade. Maris paid immediate dividends in New York, belting 39 homers, driving in a league-leading 112 runs, and was voted American League Most Valuable Player in 1960. A year later, Maris hit the jackpot in a magical 1961 baseball season, the first year of American League expansion, which lengthened the season schedule to 162 games. He teamed up with Mickey Mantle (the M&M boys) for an assault on Babe Ruth's illustrious single-season home run record of 60. M&M battled homer-for-homer through June, July, and August, but in September Mantle was felled by a leg injury and Maris was alone in the home run chase. Plagued by critics, besieged by the media, beset with stress, burdened by Major League Baseball's mandate that to be considered to have broken Ruth's record, a hitter must do it within 154 games (the number of games in a season in Ruth's day), Maris saw patches of his hair fall out. But he finally triumphed and finished with 61 homers (Mantle hit 54). Unfortunately all's well-that-ends-well wasn't true for Maris. He was excoriated in the press, charged with being uncooperative and surly, and later accused of exaggerating a hand injury. When his production fell off dramatically (13 home runs in 1966), Maris was traded to the St. Louis Cardinals for Charley Smith, a third baseman who played for the Yankees for two seasons and who, in his 10 major league seasons, hit 69 home runs, or eight more than Maris hit in that one special season.

It took the Yankees eight years to break the color line, but when they did, they chose a gem: Elston Howard, a gentleman, a man of great character, a competitor, and an outstanding ballplayer. The Yanks purchased Howard's contract from the famed Kansas Monarchs of the Negro American League when he was 21 years old. After two years in military service, Howard played a year for Kansas City in the Class AAA American Association and a year with Toronto in the Class AAA International League before coming to the Yankees to stay in 1955. With the Yankees, at first Howard was used mostly at first base and the outfield, but they tabbed him as heir apparent to Yogi Berra's catching position. By 1960, he was catching more games than Berra, and by 1961 he had taken over as the team's No. 1 catcher and hit a robust .348. In 1963, Howard was voted American League Most Valuable Player when he batted .287 with 28 home runs and 85 runs batted in. Berra and his successor Howard became the closest of friends and were practically inseparable on the road when they both served as Yankees coaches under manager Billy Martin.

Bobby Richardson was the glue of the Yankees infield in the late '50s and early '60s, a magnificent defender who won five Gold Gloves and was an outstanding clutch hitter who excelled in the World Series. While his career batting average was .266 in the regular season, he batted .305 in seven World Series. Richardson's best year was 1962, when he batted .302, led the American League in hits with 209, and had career highs in home runs with eight and RBI with 59. But Richardson is best known for two World Series moments: catching the final out of the 1963 series, a line drive off the bat of Willie McCovey of the San Francisco Giants, and setting a record with 12 RBI in the 1960 Series, for which he is the only player from a losing team to be voted World Series MVP. When his playing career of 12 seasons—all with the Yankees—ended, Richardson did some college coaching. He helped put the University of South Carolina baseball program on the map by leading the Gamecocks to the 1975 College World Series and later coached at Liberty College and Coastal Carolina. A national leader of the Fellowship of Christian Athletes, Richardson preached at the White House at the invitation of President Nixon and officiated at the funeral of his teammate and friend Mickey Mantle.

THE '70s

Thurman Munson, Roy White, Graig Nettles, Sparky Lyle
Years as Yankees Teammates—6 (1973-78)
Pennants Won as Teammates—3
World Series Won as Teammates—2

Picking fourth in baseball's 1968 amateur draft, the Yankees, in a three-year funk that saw them finish sixth, 10th, and ninth, and in need of a quick fix, could have selected Bobby Valentine, a Connecticut kid projected as a future Hall of Famer, or sluggers Greg Luzinski, Gary Matthews, or Bill Buckner. Instead they went for a catcher from Kent State University with a squatty body and a sour disposition. His name was Thurman Munson and he would change the culture around the Yankees for years to come. Rookie of the Year in 1970 and Most Valuable Player in 1976, Munson was a worthy successor to the team's long line of outstanding catchers (Bill Dickey, Yogi Berra, Elston Howard) that went back four decades. Munson was so respected by his teammates and so highly thought of by the team's owner for his competitiveness and leadership that George Steinbrenner made him the first Yankees captain since Lou Gehrig. And Munson led—with three consecutive seasons (1975–77) in which he batted at least .300 and drove in at least 100 runs, and by guiding the Yankees to three consecutive American League pennants (1976–78) and two World Series titles (1977 and '78)—until he died tragically when he crashed while practicing landing his Cessna Citation at Akron-Canton Airport on August 2, 1979. He was 32 years old.

During the team's down period in the early '60s, Yankees fans had only Mel Stottlemyre, Bobby Murcer, and Roy White to cheer for. By 1976, when the bad days finally ended and the Yankees raised one more pennant up the flag pole, Stottlemyre and Murcer were gone, but White remained. A dependable, steady, and durable (five times he played at least 155 games) switch-hitter for 15 major league seasons, all with the Yankees, White had a lifetime batting average of .271 with 160 home runs and 758 RBI and is on the Yankees' top 20 career list in games played, hits, at-bats, doubles, stolen bases, and runs.

The city of Boston's greatest gifts to the New York Yankees, a half-century apart, were George Herman "Babe" Ruth and Albert Walter "Sparky" Lyle. The return of the Yankees fortunes after a malaise of more than a decade can rightly be said to have started with the sale of the team to George Steinbrenner and the acquisition in a trade with the Red Sox of Lyle, the two events less than a year apart. Recognizing the changing nature of the game and the sudden prominence of the relief pitcher, it was manager Ralph Houk who pushed for the Yankees to get a relief specialist. Lyle was that man. In 1972, his first season as a Yankee, Lyle set the American League saves record with 35. Five years later, he won 13 games, saved 26, and became the first relief pitcher to win the Cy Young Award. In 16 seasons with five teams he would save 238 games (141 with the Yankees), pitching in an era when, at one time, the all-time saves leader was Hoyt Wilhelm, with 227. For all his success as a one-pitch pitcher (he threw only a slider), Lyle is perhaps best known for his whimsy (his favorite prank was sitting nude on birthday cakes sent to the Yankees' clubhouse) and for authoring a best-seller, *The Bronx Zoo*.

Obtaining Graig (his mother didn't like the names Craig or Greg so she combined the two) Nettles was a case of déjà vu all over again, as Yogi Berra might say. A decade earlier, after seeing Roger Maris hit home runs for the Cleveland Indians, the Yankees coveted him for his left-handed batting stroke, which they believed would make him a threat in Yankee Stadium with its short right-field porch. Now, for the same reason, they had their eye on Nettles, the Indians third baseman. The trade was made on November 27, 1972, the Yankees getting Nettles in a six-player swap. In Nettles, the Yankees got everything they bargained for, and more. In 11 seasons with the Yanks, he hit 250 home runs, including a league-leading 32 in 1976 (he would hit 390 career home runs, finishing with 333 in the American League, a league record for third basemen) and he would play a brilliant third base. In addition, Nettles brought with him a rapier wit. When Sparky Lyle was traded to Texas, Nettles quipped, "Sparky went from Cy Young to Sayonara." Discussing the chaotic state of the Yankees in the late '70s, he remarked, "Some kids grow up dreaming of playing major league baseball. Some kids grow up dreaming of joining the circus. I'm lucky. I got to do both."

20   NEW HOME

WHO MOVES INTO LUXURIOUS NEW DIGS AND THEN NEGLECTS to fill it with expensive appointment pieces?

Nobody!

And so it was that in 2009 the New York Yankees took occupancy of their opulent new residence and spent lavishly to furnish it. On December 18, 2008, they announced that they had completed two "initial" purchases, doling out $161 million (a seven-year deal) and $82.5 million (a five-year investment) for two pitchers, left-hander CC Sabathia and right-hander A.J. Burnett. Eighteen days later, on January 6, 2009, they announced an expenditure of $180 million (for eight years) for free agent first baseman Mark Teixeira, making it an outlay of $423.5 million for three pieces in a three-week shopping binge.

The official[1] opening of the new Yankee Stadium (Yankee Stadium III if you consider the original in the Bronx that opened

---

1 The unofficial opening of the new Yankee Stadium was on April 3, 2009, in an exhibition game against the Chicago Cubs. Before the official opening of their new home, the Yankees had played nine games on the road, three each at Baltimore, Kansas City, and Tampa Bay, in which they won five games and lost four.

in 1923 as Yankee Stadium I and the renovated version of same that reopened in 1976 as Yankee Stadium II) came on Thursday afternoon, April 16, 2009, with the Yankees hosting the Cleveland Indians. After 83-year-old Yankees legend and Hall of Famer Yogi Berra threw out the ceremonial first ball, the Yankees took the field with three of the new pieces in the starting lineup. Sabathia drew the honor of starting the first game in the team's new home. Teixeira played first base and batted third and Nick Swisher, who had been obtained in a trade with the Chicago White Sox on November 13, 2008, played right field and batted fourth.

The newcomers joined second baseman Robinson Cano, short-stop Derek Jeter, third baseman Cody Ransom, catcher Jorge Posada, left fielder Johnny Damon, center fielder Brett Gardner, and designated hitter Hideki Matsui in the new stadium's first starting lineup.

There was one other change. Dissatisfied with his 2008 lineup that had Damon hitting first and Jeter second, manager Joe Girardi flip-flopped the two. Batting second, Damon got the first hit in the new Yankee Stadium, a single to center field in the bottom of the first. Posada, rebounding from shoulder surgery, would hit the first home run, off Cliff Lee with two outs and nobody on base in the bottom of the fifth. At the time, it tied the score 1–1.

Sabathia left with two outs in the sixth with the score still at 1–1, but in the seventh the Indians punished the Yankees bullpen for nine runs and romped to a 10–2 victory that left an excited opening day crowd of 48,271[1] disappointed.

The newest members of the team would deliver big time all season for the Yankees and would blend seamlessly with the incumbent members of the squad. Sabathia led the pitching staff with 19 wins, tied for the league lead with Seattle's "King" Felix

---

1 For the comfort of their customers, plans called for the reduction of the seating capacity from over 57,000 in Yankee Stadium II to under 51,000 in Yankee Stadium III.

Hernandez and Detroit's Justin Verlander, and fourth in the Cy Young Award voting.

Burnett won 13 games.

Teixeira batted .292, led the league with 122 runs batted in, tied with Carlos Pena of Tampa Bay for the lead in home runs with 39, and was second to Minnesota's Joe Mauer in the Most Valuable Player voting.

Swisher contributed 29 homers and 82 RBI.

Among the holdovers, Posada, who would turn 38 on August 17 but who was healthy again, played in 111 games, 100 of them behind the plate, and batted .285 with 22 homers and 81 RBI.

Alex Rodriguez hit 30 homers and knocked in 100.

CC SABATHIA

On December 18, 2008, the Yankees made CC (it stands for Carsten Charles) Sabathia the highest paid pitcher in baseball history when they signed him as a free agent to a seven-year, $161 million contract. They later added a year for an additional $30 million. Halfway through the contract, the Yankees are satisfied that in the 6'7", 290 pound Sabathia, they got exactly what they paid for, a workhorse and an ace on their pitching staff.

Sabathia is nothing if not consistent, the true epitome of an ace. In his four years as a Yankee he has made 34, 34, 33, and 28 (he spent almost three weeks on the disabled list with elbow soreness) starts; logged 230, 237.2, 237.1, and 200 innings; won 19, 21, 19, and 15 games; had earned run averages of 3.37, 3.18, 3.00, and 3.38; winning percentages of .704, .750, .704, and .714; recorded 197, 197, 230, and 197 strikeouts; 67, 74, 61, and 44 walks; and 2, 2, 3, and 2 complete games.

Sabathia's four-year winning percentage with the Yankees of .718 puts him in first place on the team's all-time list ahead of Spud Chandler's .717.

And two members of the team's Core Four reached milestones during the 2009 season.

On June 28 in Citi Field, Mariano Rivera pitched an inning and a third in a 4–2 victory against the Mets to pick up his 18th save of the season and the 500th of his career, leaving him 71 behind Trevor Hoffman, the all-time saves leader and the only other reliever with 500 or more saves. But it wasn't the 500 milestone that gave Rivera his biggest thrill of the day. He had been credited with an RBI when he walked with the bases loaded in the top of the ninth to force home the Yankees' fourth run. It was, and remains, Rivera's only major league RBI.

Some 10 weeks later, on September 11 against the Baltimore Orioles in Yankee Stadium, Derek Jeter led off the third inning with a single to right field off O's starter Chris Tillman. It was the 2,722nd hit of his career, the most ever by a Yankee, passing the team record that Lou Gehrig had held for 72 years. (On August 16, he had passed Hall of Famer Luis Aparicio for the most hits from the shortstop position in major league history).

Girardi's switch at the top of his lineup paid huge dividends. Leading off, Jeter batted .334, third in the league to Joe Mauer and Ichiro Suzuki, and his highest average in three years (only the immortal Honus Wagner had a higher batting average for a shortstop past the age of 35); drew 72 walks, his most in four years; rapped out 212 hits, which placed him second in the league to Ichiro and boosted his career total to 2,747; scored 107 runs, tied with Damon for fourth in the league; hit 18 home runs; drove in 66 runs; had an on-base percentage of .406; and finished third in the American League Most Valuable Player voting.

In addition to his 107 runs scored, Damon had 155 hits, 63 of them for extra bases, and 71 walks. So the Yankees' top two batters were on base by walk or hit 510 times between them and combined to score 214 runs. At the age of 35, Jeter would play in 193 games, including spring training, the regular season, the postseason, the All-Star Game, and the World Baseball Classic, for which he was named captain of the United States squad by its manager, Davey Johnson.

Expressing his gratitude for his participation with the U.S. team in the World Baseball Classic, baseball commissioner Bud Selig called Jeter and followed up the telephone call with a letter in which he called the captain "Major League Baseball's foremost champion and ambassador."

In his letter of March 30, 2009, Selig wrote:

"You embody all the best of Major League Baseball. As I mentioned to you in our recent telephone conversation, you have represented the sport magnificently throughout your Hall of Fame career. On and off the field you are a man of great integrity, and you have my admiration."

Their enormous off-season investment paid off big time for the 2009 Yankees as they won 103 games, 14 more than the previous season, and moved up from third place to first, eight games ahead of the hated Red Sox, for their first division title in three years. They then made short work of the Minnesota Twins by sweeping the best-of-five Division Series three games to none.

Sabathia pitched 6⅔ powerful innings to win Game 1 by a score of 7–2, with home runs from Jeter and Matsui.

The Yankees took Game 2 in 11 innings, 4–3, with ARod tying it with a two-run blast in the ninth and Teixeira winning it with a home run leading off the bottom of the 11th. The Yankees then closed out the Twins with a 4–1 win in Game 3, as Andy Pettitte won it, Rivera saved it, and ARod and Posada belted homers.

The Los Angeles Angels of Anaheim were next for the Yankees in the American League Championship Series, a best-of-seven tournament that began in Yankee Stadium on Friday night, October 16.

The Yankees jumped out in their first at-bat, scoring twice in the bottom of the first with Jeter jump-starting the rally with a lead-off single. Five innings later, Jeter would drive in the Yankees' fourth run for a 4–1 lead. Once again, Sabathia drew the honors of opening the Series and delivered another eight dominant innings before turning it over to Rivera for the save in a 4–1 victory.

Game 2 was a 13-inning nail-biter. The score was tied 2–2 after nine. The Angels scored a run in the top of the 11th and ARod re-tied the score at 3–3 with a home run leading off the bottom of the 11th. The Yankees scored the winning run on a throwing error in the bottom of the 13th inning for a 4–3 victory and a two games to none lead in the series.

Back in Anaheim for Game 3, the Yankees and Angels played another extra-inning heart-stopper. Pettitte started for the Yankees and gave his team a chance to win, leaving in the seventh with the score tied 3–3. The Angels took the lead with a run in the seventh, but the Yankees tied it at 4–4 on Posada's home run in the eighth and the Angels won it with a run in the bottom of the 11th. The final score was 5–4, all four of the Yankees' runs coming on solo homers by Damon, Rodriguez, Jeter, and Posada.

Game 4 was the only laugher of the series. The Yankees pounded out 13 hits, including home runs by Damon and Rodriguez, for a 10–1 victory with another overpowering eight-inning effort by Sabathia, who had now started three postseason games in his first year as a Yankee and won all three.

Trailing 4–0 in Game 5, the Yankees rallied for six runs in the seventh to take a 6–4 lead. But the Angels came back with three in the bottom of the seventh to regain the lead 7–6, and that's how it ended as they returned to New York for Game 6.

It was Pettitte's turn to pitch and he turned in another work-manlike effort, leaving after 6⅓ with a 3–1 lead. Brought in for a two-inning save, Rivera was touched up for two hits and a run to cut the Yankees lead to 3–2 and give the Angels hope. But their hope was merely an illusion as the Yankees scored two in the bot-tom of the eighth and Rivera pitched a 1-2-3 ninth to nail down the 5–2 win for his third save and Pettitte's second win of the postseason.

Now it was on to the World Series, the sixth time the Core Four would play together as teammates in the World Series, a distinction held by only two other foursomes. It should not be surprising to learn that the two other foursomes to play in six World Series as teammates also were Yankees: Yogi Berra, Mickey Mantle, Whitey Ford, and Elston Howard, who played in eight World Series (1955–58 and 1960–63), and Ford, Mantle, Howard, and Bobby Richardson, teammates in seven World Series (1957–58 and 1960–64).

Providing the opposition for the Yankees in the 2009 World Series was the Philadelphia Phillies, the defending World Series champs and a powerhouse team with sluggers Ryan Howard (45 homers and a league-leading 141 RBI), Jayson Werth (36 HR and 99 RBI), Raul Ibanez (34 HR and 93 RBI), and Chase Utley (31 HR and 93 RBI).

With a combined 468 home runs between them (the Phillies had led the National League with 224 homers and the Yankees led the American League with 244), the 2009 World Series figured to be a slugfest pairing two teams that last met in the World Series in 1950. In the 59 years since that meeting the Phillies had reached the World Series only four times and won it twice.

To open the 2009 World Series in Yankee Stadium on October 28, the Yankees, as usual, sent their new man, the big guy, 6'7" and 290 (or more) pounds, CC Sabathia, to the mound. This time, however, CC was grabbed by the law of averages and he was out-pitched by Cliff Lee, who stifled the Yankees on six hits, three by Derek Jeter, struck out 10, and went the distance in a 6–1 victory. Give Round 1 of this heavyweight slugfest to the Phillies on the strength of two home runs off the bat of Chase Utley, both of them against Sabathia.

The Yankees got even in Game 2 with A.J. Burnett pitching seven innings for the win, allowing four hits and striking out nine. Mariano Rivera pitched two innings for the save and Teixeira and Matsui each hit solo homers in the 3–1 victory.

Although playing at home and out-homering the Yankees four homers to three, the Phillies lost back-to-back games, 8–5 on Saturday, October 31, and 7–4 on Sunday, November 1, to fall behind in the Series, three games to one. Pettitte went six innings to win Game 3 and Joba Chamberlain, in relief of Sabathia, got the win in Game 4, with Rivera pitching a perfect ninth for the save.

The Phillies saved face with their fans by taking Game 5 at Citizens Bank Park 8–6, and thereby avoiding the embarrassment of watching the Yankees celebrate their World Series victory on the Phillies' home field. That only delayed the inevitable. Two days later, in Yankee Stadium, the Yankees completed their mission with a 7–3 victory.

It was altogether fitting that in the clinching game, Andy Pettitte, the third oldest Yankee, was the winning pitcher, with Jorge Posada, the second oldest Yankee, as his catcher, and Mariano Rivera, the oldest Yankee, pitching the final inning and two thirds. In 16 innings in the postseason, Rivera allowed just one run while collecting five saves.

The Phillies out-slugged the Yankees 11 home runs (five by Utley) to six, but the Yankees had Pettitte, who won two games, and Rivera, who saved two.

Their almost half billion–dollar investment had paid off for the Yankees with the 27th World Series championship in their history, but their first in nine years.

The "Core Four" of Mariano Rivera, Andy Pettitte, Jorge Posada, and Derek Jeter had earned its fifth World Series ring and would enjoy, one more time, their trip through New York City's Canyon of Heroes.

21   BYE BYE ANDY

THERE WAS A GATHERING AT YANKEE STADIUM ON FEBRUARY 4, 2011, of media, team brass, employees, and selected friends, all of them summoned to witness the breakup of the Core Four.

Andy Pettitte was leaving the Yankees. Again! Only this time, he wasn't moving to another team in another league in another state some 1,700 miles away. This time, Andy Pettitte was retiring to spend more time with his wife and their four school-age children. He had made his decision and it was definite, final, and irrevocable.

Flash back to 2007. Having completed his three-year free agent commitment to the Houston Astros, Pettitte opted not to return to the Astros and came back to the Yankees as a free agent. Over the next three seasons, he won 43 games and lost 31. In 2009, despite a 14–8 record in the regular season, he excelled in the postseason with a perfect 4–0 record, including victories in Game 3 of the World Series against the Phillies and the Game 6 clincher.

In 2010, Pettitte got off to the best start of his career. By mid-July, a month after his 38th birthday, Pettitte had a record of 11–2, an earned run average of 2.70, and was on pace for his first 20-win season in seven years when he suffered a groin strain that would sideline him for two months. He returned in September to make three starts and he would not win another game. But he was ready for the postseason.

He pitched seven innings against the Minnesota Twins in Game 2 of the Division Series and was the winner in a 5–2 victory. Mariano Rivera got the save, the 10th time Rivera and Pettitte had partnered on a postseason win. (Rivera would save 68 of the 203 regular season victories Pettitte accumulated as a Yankee, the most of any starter/closer team in baseball history.)

Pettitte pitched Game 3 of the 2010 American League Championship Series against the Texas Rangers and again was effective, but this time he ran up against a red-hot Cliff Lee. Pettitte left after seven innings trailing 2–0, a game the Rangers eventually won 8–0.

With his groin strain completely healed, Pettitte pitched well and could have continued to pitch in 2011, but after much deliberation decided to call it a career. To clear his head and think about his future, Pettitte went alone to his ranch in a remote part of Texas, four hours away from his home. He told the assemblage at the Yankee Stadium press conference on February 4, 2011, it was on his drive home that he came to a decision.

"When I got by myself and thought about it, I said 'I'm going to play. The fans, the Yankees, need me to play. My wife supports it, my kids support it. I'm going to play.' But when I dug deep down and did some soul-searching, I don't know how to explain it; it wasn't there. It just didn't feel right for me anymore. I didn't have the hunger, the drive that I felt I needed.

"My arm feels great, my body feels great. I've been working out extremely hard for about the last three and a half weeks, and I know my body would get to where it needs to be. But my heart's not where it needs to be."

Yankees general manager Brian Cashman, whose job it was going to be to find a replacement to fill Pettitte's spot in the starting rotation, was lavish in his praise of the left-hander.

"He's going to be tough to replace, clearly, on the mound" Cashman said. "But he's going to be even tougher to replace in the clubhouse, because he's been a glue guy. He's been a guy that, whatever another teammate is going through, he's going to be there and help them through it and be there for them."

No other member of the Yankees Core Four attended Pettitte's press conference, but two of them were contacted and bid their teammate and fellow Core Four member a fond farewell.

Rivera: "Andy was a great teammate and a wonderful guy. He was a fighter and all about winning, and he was respected by every person in the clubhouse."

Posada: "I'm really sad that Andy is going to retire. He was so much more than a teammate to me; he was one of my closest friends. I admire everything that he has accomplished as a Yankee, but Andy was someone who always put the team first. I'm going to miss him deeply."

It was hardly surprising that, even in an emotional and celebratory occasion, someone would raise the question of Pettitte's involvement in baseball's ongoing substance abuse problem. Pettitte's name had come up in the Mitchell Report (The Report to the Commissioner of Baseball of an Independent Investigation into the Illegal Use of Steroids and Other Performance Enhancing Substances by Players in Major League Baseball, a 409-page report of a 21-month investigation headed up by former United States Senator from Maine, George J. Mitchell).

Pettitte, who admitted taking human growth hormone twice, in 2002 and 2004 (he said he took HGH not to get a competitive edge, but to speed up recovery from an elbow injury in order to return and help his team), was scheduled later in the year to testify as a government witness in the perjury trial of his former friend and teammate, Roger Clemens. He was asked if that had any impact on his decision to retire.

"None, zero," he replied. "I would never let that interfere with a life decision that I'm going to make for me and my family."

And so Andy Pettitte faded into retirement, taking with him 240 victories in 17 seasons with two teams, the New York Yankees and the Houston Astros, a .635 winning percentage, a 3.88 earned run average, 19 postseason wins, five World Series rings, and a solemn vow.

"I can tell you one thing: I am not going to play this season. I can tell you that 100 percent. But I guess you can never say never. If my stomach was just churning once Opening Day started, and I'm like, 'Oh my gosh, I've made a huge mistake,' and I've felt like that the whole season, I can't say that I wouldn't consider coming back. But I can tell you right now I'd be embarrassed because of what I've done."

22 JORGE'S REBELLION

FOR 16 YEARS, JORGE POSADA HAD BEEN THE MOST LOYAL OF employees, a good soldier, the ultimate competitor, the consummate team player. He had always done as he was asked, never questioned authority, swallowed his pride, suppressed his ego, sacrificed his body, played through pain—all for the good of the team.

Now, after so many productive, borderline Hall of Fame seasons, Jorge Posada was being disrespected, insulted, put upon, taken advantage of, in danger of being held up to ridicule, losing face, all of his past achievements forgotten and dismissed with a wave of the hand and the stroke of a pen.

Jorge Posada was as mad as hell and he wasn't going to take it anymore!

The first sign of trouble in Paradise, Bronx division, came in the off-season between the 2010 and 2011 baseball seasons. In 2010 Posada, at age 38, had batted .248, hit 18 home runs, and driven in 57, which represented a decline from the previous season of 37 batting points, four home runs, and 24 RBI. He had appeared in 120 games, but only 83 behind the plate, as Francisco Cervelli began getting more playing time at catcher as the season wore on.

Posada's contract was due to lapse after the 2011 season and he hoped for an offer that would extend his career, but when that failed to come, combined with his advanced age and reduced playing time, Posada could clearly read the handwriting on the wall. To add to his dismay, he was informed after the 2010 season by general manager Brian Cashman that in '11 Posada would be used exclusively as a designated hitter and that he would no longer be a catcher, except in the direst emergency.

It was a blow to his pride, but one Posada sucked up with a personal vow to be such a productive DH that the team would have no choice but to return him to his natural habitat behind the plate. It was wishful thinking on Posada's part. It never happened.

He started the season well enough, 4-for-14 with three home runs and six RBI in his first four games, and then came the decline, slowly at first and then precipitously.

On May 14, the Yankees were in Boston preparing to face the Red Sox in the second game of a three-game series. The Yanks had lost three straight to fall to 20–16, which left them in second place, two games behind the Tampa Bay Rays, and Posada was mired in a severe slump. His average had plummeted to a microscopic .165 with six homers and 15 RBI. What's more, he was hitless in 24 at-bats against left-handers, making it difficult for manager Joe Girardi to justify using the veteran as a right-handed batter.

On this Saturday, however, the Red Sox's scheduled pitcher was right-hander Josh Beckett, so Posada had every reason to believe he would be in the starting lineup as he followed his normal routine of arriving at the ballpark several hours before the start of the night game and checking the lineup card that had been made out by Girardi.

When he did so, and found his name, Posada was stunned. He was in the lineup, all right, but he was listed in the ninth batting position, which he considered an unforgivable slight. He hadn't batted ninth since early in the 1999 season, before he had become an All-Star.

Several emotions coursed through Posada. Not only did he feel hurt and disrespected, he wondered if this was payback. He and Girardi had never been close, much of their coolness toward each other dated back to the late 1990s, when Posada was the up-and-coming future star being primed to take away Girardi's job as the Yankees starting catcher.

Instead of confronting Girardi to seek an explanation for this decision, Posada chose another way to express his displeasure. He marched into the manager's office and told Girardi he was unable to play.

Girardi characterized their conversation as "really short." Girardi said, "He came into my office and said he needed a day, he couldn't DH today. That was basically the extent of the conversation."

According to Posada, "I told him I couldn't play today and that I needed time to…first to clear my head. That was it. My back stiffened up a little bit. I was taking a lot of ground balls at first base and worked out, and I wasn't 100 percent."

You couldn't find anyone who bought into Posada's explanation. For one thing, baseball protocol normally dictates that a player report any physical ailment to the trainer, who in turn passes along the information to the manager and/or the general manager. Posada never talked with the Yankees trainers. They, like everyone else, knew nothing of the catcher's stiff back. Cashman, traveling with the team, said he knew nothing of Posada's back stiffness and Girardi said Posada never mentioned a problem with his back when Jorge was in the manager's office.

Plain and simple, Posada was in a snit over being put in the No. 9 batting position. He was pouting. He was mad as hell and he wasn't going to take it anymore!

When reporters, who had seen the original lineup with Posada in it, wondered why he had been scratched, Cashman had no choice but to address the issue. During the third inning, he met with reporters and said that to his knowledge, Posada did not have an injury.

"I don't know why he made a statement during the game," said Posada. "I don't understand that. That's the way he works now, I guess. I think he should have waited for the game to be over to talk to whoever. You don't do that. You're not supposed to do that."

Cashman said he had told Posada and his agent that he was going to address the media and exactly what he was going to say when he did.

Not surprisingly, Posada's action received the support of his teammates, and even of his opponents.

Yankees captain and Posada's best friend, Derek Jeter, said the catcher owed no one an apology for asking out of the game.

"If he said he needed a day to clear his mind, there's no need to apologize," Jeter said. "I think everybody understands that. I think everybody in here [the clubhouse] understands that sometimes this game can be tough on you mentally. Everybody's struggled, everybody's been in a situation where things don't seem to be clicking the right way. And if that's the reason why he came out, then he doesn't need apologize."

David Ortiz, "Big Papi" of the Red Sox, also saw things Posada's way.

"They're doing that guy wrong," said Ortiz, like Posada, confined to being a designated hitter. "They're doing him wrong. You know why? That guy, he is legendary right there in that organization. And dude, DH-ing sucks. DH-ing is not easy."

Red Sox captain Jason Varitek, like Posada a switch-hitter and only eight months younger than his longtime contemporary and catching rival, was asked if he could appreciate Posada's frustration.

"We're dealing with a lot of speculation right now with the little bit I just heard," Varitek said. "I do know and respect what the man has done behind the plate for many, many years. Like I do with most things, I'm going to wait for the truth to come out and I'm not going to respond to something on hearsay."

With 24 hours and a night's sleep, Posada's temperature had cooled somewhat. He went into Girardi's office the day after the brouhaha and apologized, sort of.

"I just had a bad day," he said.

The conversation between Posada and Girardi then evolved into a clear-the-air discussion of their relationship, which Girardi could sense was rather emotional for Posada. What he saw, said the manager, "was not your typical Jorge Posada face."

Girardi said he told Posada, "I just want to see you have joy, and I want to see you enjoy what you're doing and enjoy the game of baseball like you've always loved it. That's more important to me than the apology."

Recalling his feelings during the time when he was trying to hang on to his job and Posada was coming on fast to take it away, Girardi said, "I knew that he was a better player than I was. There would be days I would get two hits and I'd go look at the lineup and his name would be there and I didn't necessarily like it, but I understood it. Jorge was a more talented player, and I moved on, but it wasn't the first time I had to move on because someone was more talented. It was the reality of the situation, and Jorge's been a great Yankee.

"He's done so many wonderful things for this organization, and I'm extremely proud of what he's done and to know Jorgie, and you look back, everything that we've done. I just said, 'I know this is hard, I know it's hard to struggle, but you'll get through this.'"

Speaking to reporters, Posada was in a more conciliatory mood the day after his blowup.

"You learn from your mistakes, and I think I'll learn from this," he said. "Everybody has a bad day. I think I just had one yesterday and I'll try to move on."

Posada also extended an olive branch in the form of an apology to general manager Brian Cashman, who would have been within his contractual rights to fine or suspend Posada. He did neither and said he considered the matter closed.

Posada was not in the starting lineup in the third game of the series against the Red Sox, but that was not punitive. Boston's pitcher was left-hander Jon Lester and Posada's ineptitude as a right-handed batter made it an easy decision for Girardi to use right-handed hitting Andruw Jones as the designated hitter against Lester. But when Jones was due to bat in the eighth inning against right-hander Daniel Bard, Girardi called him back and sent Posada up as a pinch hitter. He drew a walk.

After the unpleasantness in Boston, Posada picked it up somewhat and finished the season with a .235 average, 14 home runs, and 44 RBI—fairly respectable numbers for only 344 at-bats—helping the Yankees win their 12th division title in 16 years, all of them with Posada on the roster.

However, the Yankees faltered in the postseason and were eliminated in the first round when they were beaten by the Detroit Tigers in five games. Posada held up his end. He started all five games and batted .429 on six hits in 14 at-bats.

It was his last hurrah. When the season ended, there was no offer for the 2012 season, not from the Yankees or any other team. Reluctantly, Posada announced his retirement.

23   CLOSURE

ON MONDAY SEPTEMBER 19, 2011, MARIANO RIVERA PITCHED a perfect ninth inning—he retired Trevor Plouffe on a ground ball to second baseman Robinson Cano, got Michael Cuddyer on a line drive to right fielder Chris Dickerson, and with his signature cutter struck out Chris Parmelee looking—in the Yankees 6–4 win over the Minnesota Twins in Yankee Stadium to record his 43rd save of the season and the 602nd of his career, passing Trevor Hoffman, since retired, for the most saves in baseball history.

The monumental achievement earned the usual excitement and homage from the crowd of 40,045; elicited a congratulatory telephone call from the president of Panama, Ricardo Martinelli (if you're the president of Panama and you want to continue being the president of Panama, you had better cozy up to Mariano Rivera lest he chooses to run for the office himself); and set off a raging debate.

Is Rivera, as many have contended, the greatest closer in baseball history?

Some say the greatest closer in baseball history was Cy Young, who pitched 749 complete games in his career, 103 more than any other pitcher. (Rivera has finished more games than any pitcher in history, 892).

Some say Mariano Rivera is the greatest closer of only the last 30 years, which is about the time the term "closer" entered the baseball lexicon. Before then, relief pitchers were not called closers and were not used in the same manner that closers are used today.

Rich "Goose" Gossage, who saved 310 games with nine different teams in 22 major league seasons (from 1972 to 1994, with one year spent in Japan) and was elected to the Hall of Fame in 2008, has been the most vocal proponent of the difference between the role of the "closer" in his day and Rivera's.

The basic difference, Gossage points out, is that today's closer routinely enters a game to start the ninth inning with a lead of three runs or less, nobody out and nobody on base, while in Gossage's day and before, it was common for the reliever (closer?) to come into a game in the ninth inning, the eighth, the seventh and, occasionally, even as early as the sixth, and with runners on base. A check of the seasons of some of the great relief pitchers of the past in comparison with Rivera makes Gossage's point emphatically while, at the same time, gives a thumbnail history of the evolution of the relief pitcher as closer.

(It's important to note that the save didn't become an official statistic of Major League Baseball until 1969. Prior to that year, there was no such thing as a save, though there were relief pitchers that arrived late in a game and finished up in a winning effort. It was therefore left to statisticians to research every game ever played and, using today's requirements, tabulate the saves that would have been credited.)

PITCHER	SEASON	SAVES	GAMES	IP	IP/G
Johnny Murphy	1939	19	38	61⅓	1.6
Joe Page	1949	27	60	135⅓	2.3
Ryne Duren	1958	20	44	75⅔	1.7
Luis Arroyo	1961	29	65	119	1.8
Elroy Face	1962	28	62	92	1.5
Hoyt Wilhelm	1965	20	66	144	2.2
Sparky Lyle	1972	35	59	107⅔	1.8
Mike Marshall	1974	21	106	208⅓	1.9
Rollie Fingers	1978	28	67	107⅓	1.6
Goose Gossage	1980	33	64	99	1.5
Bruce Sutter	1984	45	71	122⅔	1.7
Dennis Eckersley	1992	51	69	80	1.2
Mariano Rivera	2011	43	64	61⅓	0.9

"When you come into the game with inherited runners, when you can't even allow the ball to be put in play, that's where I shined," Gossage told *The New York Times*. "I used to love that. I could get two strikeouts. The mental strain is incredible. I would be exhausted just because of the letdown of the pressure and the mental part of it.

"When I pitched the ninth inning to save a three-run lead, coming in with no one on base, I felt guilty. I would go home and be embarrassed. Rivera is an awesome pitcher, but what he's doing is easy. What he does and what we used to do is apples and oranges. It's not fair to compare what closers today do with what we did. Managers today go by a big bible of how to use relievers. Righty faces righty. Lefty faces lefty. Face one batter. Don't use a closer more than one inning. They use three guys now—two set-up guys and a closer—to do what we used to do by ourselves.

"They'd put me in when we were losing by a run and there were men on base because they needed to get that out. If we had a three-run lead going into the ninth, they didn't even put me in. Anyone can finish that. Today, if a closer comes in in the eighth inning, it makes headlines. It's embarrassing."

Without the benefit of sabermetrics and computers, managers in Gossage's day and before were not as enlightened as they are today. Needless to say, Gossage believes that had he been used in his day as closers are used today, he might have been a member of the 600 saves club along with Rivera and Hoffman.

"Four or five of us in the past would have gotten there if we'd have been used the way they use these guys now, just to get saves," he said.

Even Rivera's remarkable postseason record has its detractors. They point out that because of the expanded playoffs, Rivera has had many more opportunities to compete than his predecessors. That's true (Murphy, Page, Duren, Arroyo, Face, and Wilhelm had only the World Series; Marshall and Sutter only the World Series and League Championship Series), but look at the results Rivera has compiled in the most pressurized situations: eight wins, 42 saves, a 0.70 earned run average, 110 strikeouts, 21 walks, 86 hits, and 13 runs in 96 games covering 141 innings. In those 96 postseason games and 141 innings through 2012, he has allowed only two home runs, to Sandy Alomar Jr. of the Cleveland Indians in Game 4 of the 1997 ALCS and to Jay Payton of the New York Mets in Game 2 of the 2000 World Series. Put another way, since yielding his last postseason home run, he has gone 57 games, 81⅓ innings, 304 batters, and 1,140 pitches *without* giving up a home run.

Thirty one of Rivera's 42 postseason saves were for more than one inning, including four seven-out saves in which he wasn't charged with a run and didn't allow an inherited runner to score.

Rivera has had 29 two-inning appearances in the postseason, with four wins, 14 saves, and three holds.

The true genius of Mariano Rivera lies in his ability to accomplish so much while ostensibly throwing only one pitch, the cut fastball (or cutter), a pitch thrown with the similar motion and the same velocity as a fastball but as it approaches the hitter it bores in...in...*in*...on a left-handed batter and away...away...*away*... from a right-handed batter. It has wrought a forest of broken bats. In the 2001 season alone, Rivera is said to have broken 44 bats, but who's counting?

As Yankees hitting instructor Kevin Long explained to *The New York Times*, when Rivera throws his cutter "You're thinking it's going to be right here [he motions to the middle of home plate], so you start to swing and it ends up here [he motions to a spot on the fist of a left-handed hitter, a movement of some six to eight inches]. You might know it's going to cut, but you really can't see it until the last minute, when it takes off."

Eric Chavez has had the rare dual experience of hitting against the Mariano Rivera cutter as a member of the Oakland Athletics and watching him throw it to hitters from his third-base vantage point as a teammate.

"When you go back and look at his career and what he's done with that one pitch, I don't think there's a greater achievement than that," Chavez said. "To go through major league hitters and dominate for all those years, it's one of the greatest feats I'll ever look back on. I don't think people realize how incredible it really is. It will never be duplicated, ever."

The cutter is Mariano Rivera's signature pitch, "The single best pitch ever in the game," said 600–home run–slugger Jim Thome. "A buzzsaw," said Atlanta Braves future–Hall of Famer Chipper Jones. "You know what's coming," said Mike Sweeney, a five-time All-Star and a lifetime .297 hitter for 16 major league seasons, "but you know what's coming in horror films, too. It still gets you."

It's a pitch so dominant, so admired, so feared, and so closely identified with and perfected by one pitcher it would not be surprising that in the not too distant future managers, coaches, pitchers, broadcasters, and baseball writers will refer to the pitch not as "the cutter," but as "the Mariano" or "the Mo" or "the Rivera," much in the way that ulnar collateral ligament reconstruction is commonly known as "Tommy John surgery."

Rivera's genius also is in his amazing pinpoint control, the velocity he generates from a trim, athletic, 6'2", 185-pound body, and a smooth, fluid pitching motion that allows him to repeat his delivery pitch after pitch, along with his durability and his longevity.

Since 1996, and until May 3, 2012, five months and four days after his 42nd birthday (when he tore the anterior cruciate ligament in his right knee shagging fly balls in Kansas City prior to a game, as he had done maybe a few thousand times), Rivera had pitched in fewer than 60 games twice and fewer than 50 just once.

By comparison, Joe Page retired at age 32, tried a comeback four years later, and pitched in only seven games with the Pirates. Bruce Sutter and Ryne Duren were finished at age 35, Luis Arroyo at 36, Sparky Lyle at 37, Johnny Murphy, Mike Marshall, and Rollie Fingers at 38.

Elroy Face pitched until 1969, when, at the age of 41, he won four games and saved five for the Montreal Expos. At the age of 41, Rivera won one game and saved 44.

Goose Gossage pitched until the age of 42, but managed only one save and hadn't saved as many as 13 games since age 36.

Hoyt Wilhelm was a physical phenomenon. At the age of 47, he recorded 13 saves. At the age of 49, he had a record of 0–1 with one save for the Los Angeles Dodgers and he made his last appearance 16 days before his 50th birthday. Wilhelm's longevity may have been aided by the fact he threw a trick pitch, the knuckleball, which was more baffling to hitters and less stressful on the arm of the pitcher.

The only reliever on the list who rivaled Rivera in both dominance and longevity is also the only one whose career overlapped with Rivera's: Dennis Eckersley. Eckersley saved 36 games at the age of 42 and retired at 43 after posting a record of 4–1 with one save for the Boston Red Sox. (P.S. Eckersley, Gossage, Sutter, Wilhelm, and Fingers are the only relief pitchers that have been elected to the Hall of Fame.)

It's worth noting, and quite obvious, that most of the relievers mentioned above were merely hanging on at the end, eking out another contract or two, bouncing around from team to team. There has been no hanging around for Mariano Rivera, no bouncing around from team to team, no eking out another contract or two. He is the only reliever on the above list that has played his entire career for just one team.

Through it all, Rivera typically has carefully avoided involving himself in the debate about the difference between past relievers and today's closers. He is not known to even be quoted on the subject. After all, the claim that he is greatest closer in baseball history was not his claim, the rules for saves are not his rules, and the manner in which he is used has not been dictated by him. It's the manager, not the pitcher, that decides how a closer is to be used.

There is a school of thought that contends if Goose Gossage were pitching under today's conditions and philosophy, he would have as many saves as Mariano Rivera.

Maybe!

WHAT THEY SAY ABOUT MARIANO RIVERA

Joe Torre, on ESPN radio the day after Rivera went down with a torn ACL in his left knee: "During the course of the season your players that play every day are probably more valuable, but when you get into the postseason, that last inning is so valuable, those last three outs. I laugh because I have been listening to the radio today and I've laughed at some people when it's suggested that he may be not only one of the best relievers but maybe one of the best pitchers, and they say, 'Well you only pitch one inning so how can you say that?' Those last three outs, unless you sit in the dugout or you've watched it for years, those last three outs are like gold. I don't think there's any question of how valuable he was and in the postseason I don't think there was anyone more important."

Tom Kelly, former manager of the Minnesota Twins: "He needs to pitch in a higher league, if there is one. Ban him from baseball. He should be illegal."

Hall of Fame closer Dennis Eckersley: "[Rivera is] the best ever, no doubt."

Trevor Hoffman, runner-up to Rivera as the all-time career leader in saves: "[Rivera] will go down as the best reliever in the game in history."

More Joe Torre: "He's the best I've ever been around. Not only the ability to pitch and perform under pressure, but the calm he puts over the clubhouse."

Alex Rodriguez: "He's the only guy in baseball who can change the game from a seat in the clubhouse or the bullpen. He would start affecting teams as early as the fifth inning because they knew he was out there. I've never seen anyone who could affect a game like that. He's the greatest weapon in modern baseball, the greatest I've ever seen or played against."

Michael Young: "I respect Mo more than anybody in the game. The guy goes out there and gets three outs and shakes Posada's hand. You appreciate someone who respects the game like he does, respects the people he plays with and against, and obviously his results speak for themselves."

Joe Girardi: "He's sneaky. Because he's small, and because his delivery is so free and easy, so smooth, his stuff doesn't look as if it's coming at you as fast as it is. Then it's by you."

Mark Teixeira: "I have always argued that he is the best *pitcher* of all time, not a reliever, the best pitcher of all time."

Joe Nathan, Texas Rangers closer: "I look up to how he's handled himself on and off the field. You never see him show up anyone and he respects the game. I've always looked up to him and it's always a compliment to be just mentioned in the same sentence as him."

Derek Jeter: "He's the best. I don't care how many saves [other closers] have. I think you have to put him at the top of the list. [He is] a once-in-a-lifetime player [and] the most mentally tough [teammate he's ever played with]."

Mariano Rivera: "I get the ball, I throw the ball, and then I take a shower."

24   HIT MAN

ONCE HE PASSED LOU GEHRIG FOR THE MOST HITS BY A YANKEE at 2,722, the countdown was on for Derek Jeter to reach the magic milestone number of 3,000, which had been achieved by only 27 players in baseball history.

While becoming the Yankees' all-time hits leader, Jeter's season average of .334 and his total of 212 hits were his highest in three years. It also was seen by many as the calm before the storm.

In 2010, Jeter's average would plummet by 64 points to .270, the lowest of his career if you don't include his .250 average when he was brought up for 15 games at the end of the 1995 season. Despite playing in 157 games, the third most of his career, he had only 179 hits, his fewest in seven years, and a career low (again, not including his cameo appearance in 1995) 10 home runs.

Some said his batting decline was caused by the stress of the chase for 3,000 hits. Others saw a more practical explanation: his age! On June 26 he had turned 36 years old, an age when most players are well into their physical and statistical descent—especially shortstops, the only defensive position Jeter has ever played. (Of the 2,295 games in which he had appeared, 2,276 were at shortstop; the other 19 were as a designated hitter.)

His critics attacked not only his hitting, but his fielding. He had lost a few steps, they charged. He no longer was the offensive force who had earned four Silver Slugger Awards (presented to the outstanding hitter at each position), or the lithe and agile shortstop who had earned four Gold Gloves (he would win his fifth that season). Move him down in the batting order, they urged. Find another defensive position for him, they implored.

Jeter heard all the comments about his age. He knew about the remarks from radio talk show hosts and their callers, and read the stories by baseball writers that he had lost a step, or two, or three, in the field, and of his diminished power at bat. Even if he hadn't heard the comments, or listened to the radio, or read the papers, he would have been reminded by reports, in the midst of negotiations between Jeter and the Yankees on a new contract, that some members of the team's hierarchy were questioning whether Jeter's skills were eroding and suggested he might be best served if he explored free agency. Those negotiations got ugly at times, but fearing a public backlash should they allow the popular team captain to walk, the Yankees eventually grudgingly caved in and signed Jeter to a three-year $51 million extension. With his new contract that would take him through the 2013 season, Jeter set about putting the scurrilous stories of his demise to rest.

Despite his determination, Jeter got the 2011 season off to an alarmingly slow start. On April 20, although he had passed Al Simmons, Rogers Hornsby, "Wee" Willie Keeler, Jake Beckley, and Barry Bonds on the hit ladder on his way to 3,000, he was batting a paltry .219, giving credence to the widely held belief that the captain of the Yankees, like an old soldier, was fading.

Still, the pursuit of 3,000 continued. On April 24, he passed Frank Robinson. On May 10, he passed "Wahoo" Sam Crawford. On June 7, he passed Sam Rice.

By June 13, he had raised his average to a respectable if un-Jeter-like .260 and was 28th on baseball's all-time hits list with 2,994, just six away from the promised land, when he suffered a calf injury that would delay his 3,000-hit coronation and land him on the disabled list for the first time in eight years.

While the recovery and rehab in Tampa was a drag for Jeter, who hated being sidelined and throughout his career was known for playing hurt, it also may have been a blessing in disguise. It gave him an opportunity to get together with hitting instructor Gary Denbo, Jeter's first professional manager. The two worked diligently for hours each day attempting to replicate and recapture the batting style that made Jeter so successful. The layoff also allowed him to clear his head, escape the pressure of the chase for 3,000, and return to the Yankees rested and refreshed.

It was a different Derek Jeter—or rather, it was the old, pre-2010 Derek Jeter—who rejoined the Yankees in Cleveland on July 4. Needing to shake the rust of a month-long layoff, he was hit-less in four at-bats in his first game back, but the next day he had two hits and another one the day after that, leaving him three hits short of 3,000, with a good chance he would reach the milestone at Yankee Stadium during a four-game series against the Tampa Bay Rays. Perfect!

The four games against Tampa Bay would be Jeter's last chance to reach the 3,000-hit mark in front of the home fans. After that series, the Yanks were scheduled to play eight games on the road, four in Toronto and four at Tampa Bay.

Hit No. 2,998 for Jeter came in the first game of the series against Tampa Bay on Thursday night, July 7, a line-drive double into the left-center-field gap leading off the bottom of the first inning on the first pitch from 6'9" right-hander Jeff Neimann. Jeter would bat four more times in the game but failed to get another hit.

It rained in New York on Friday, July 8, a torrential downpour causing the game between the Yankees and Rays to be postponed. Fearing that a reduction of the Tampa Bay series from four games to three because of the postponement would damage Jeter's chances of getting his 3,000th hit at Yankee Stadium, the Yankees asked the Rays for permission to play a day-night doubleheader the next day. The Rays refused, which was their right according to the Collective Bargaining Agreement between Major League Baseball owners and players.

Tampa Bay manager Joe Maddon said he thought Jeter wasn't going to need the fourth game to reach the milestone.

"He looks very spiffy to me right now," Maddon said. "Well-rested after his injury. I can see the eagerness. He looks good. I think he looks really good. So there's probably a pretty good shot it's going to happen within the next few days."

Color Joe Maddon clairvoyant!

Saturday afternoon, July 9, came up sun-splashed, hot, and humid in the Bronx. In Yankee Stadium there was an air of excitement and the buzz of anticipation as the Yankees prepared to take on the Tampa Bay Rays. Leading off the bottom of the first, Derek Jeter, still hitting just .257, worked the count to 3–2 against the Rays' ace, left-hander David Price, and then hit a ground ball through the left side. Hit No. 2,999.

That hit, Jeter said, helped him to relax. "It was huge," he said. "He could have thrown it in the dugout and I would have swung. I was not trying to walk."

Jeter came to bat again in the third inning. The Rays had scored a run in the second to take a 1–0 lead. Brett Gardner started the bottom of the third by grounding out to second base. Again Jeter worked the count to 3–2. Price, whose fastball has been clocked occasionally at 100 miles per hour, figured Jeter would be sitting on his fastball. He threw a curveball; Jeter swung. His bat hitting the ball made a resounding crack that reverberated throughout the cavernous stadium and the ball soared high and far to left field before disappearing into the seats.

Derek Jeter, who had hit only two home runs up to that game, who hadn't hit a home run in 100 at-bats, had entered the 3,000-hit club, put his shoulder to the door of that exclusive chamber and pushed his way in with a home run.

The Yankee Stadium clock read 2:00.

The game was tied 1–1.

The fans, 48,103 strong, chanted "DER-ek JEE-ter…DER-ek JEE-ter!"

Jorge Posada, his best friend on the team, led the charge of Yankees from the dugout to mob their captain, the conquering hero, and smother him with hugs and pats on the back.

The charge to the plate, said Posada, was spontaneous. "Everybody ran out there and gave him a big hug. I told him I was proud of him. I got a little emotional because I was so happy for him."

Members of the rival Tampa Bay Rays, led by Jeter's former teammate, Johnny Damon, applauded the newest member of the 3,000-hit club and tipped their caps.

The game was delayed for four minutes as the crowd went wild and Jeter acknowledged the cheers by taking a curtain call and raising his fists.

Derek Jeter had become the 28th member of baseball's 3,000-hit club, and the first to join since Craig Biggio of the Houston Astros in 2007.

He was the 11th member to get all 3,000 hits with the same team.

He was the first Yankee to be admitted to that club.

He was the first to get his 3,000th hit in Yankee Stadium, new or old.

He joined Wade Boggs as the only members to hit a home run for No. 3,000.

At 37 years, 13 days old, he was the fourth-youngest player to reach 3,000 hits, behind Ty Cobb, Hank Aaron, and Robin Yount.

Hit No. 3,000 came in Jeter's 2,362nd game, which was the seventh fastest in baseball history, and in his 9,604th at-bat, which was 10th fastest in baseball history.

Getting 3,000 hits "means a lot," said Jeter. "It's a number that has meant a lot in the history of the game because not too many people have done it before. To be the only Yankee to do it…to be the only Yankee to do anything…is pretty special."

Jeter called the events of the afternoon "one of those special days" and confessed to fibbing in the days leading up to this climactic event.

"I've been lying for a long time saying I wasn't nervous and there was no pressure," he said. "I felt a lot of pressure to do it here while we're at home. You try not to think about it, but who are we kidding? Everywhere I went, somebody wanted to talk about it."

Said David Price: "I didn't really care if he got it off me, as long as he didn't drive in a run or score a run, and he did all those things in that one at-bat. Good for him."

Jeter had reached his primary goal, but he wasn't finished for the day. There still was work to be done, a game to play, a game to win, and, with the Yankees starting the day a game behind the first place Red Sox, an important game at that.

In the fifth inning, with the Rays leading 3–2, Jeter led off by hitting Price's first pitch for a double down the left-field line—hit No. 3,001!—that jump-started a two-run rally to put the Yankees ahead 4–3.

In the sixth, with two out and a runner on first, he hit took a 1–0 pitch from reliever Brandon Gomes, and with his familiar, patented inside-out swing, lined a single to right field for hit No. 3,002.

And in the eighth, with the score tied 4–4 and Joel Peralta on the mound for Tampa Bay, Eduardo Nunez led off with a double, Brett Gardner sacrificed him to third, and Jeter singled to center for his fifth hit of the game, the 3,003[rd] hit of his career, joining Craig Biggio as the only players to have five hits in a game on the day they reached the 3,000-hit plateau, and driving Nunez in for what would be the winning run.

A perfect ending to a perfect day!

Mariano Rivera said the only thing that surprised him about the day was that Jeter didn't hit a triple to go along with his single, double, and home run to complete the cycle.

"The best thing for him is how he prepares himself day in and day out," said Rivera. "He has done it for years. I am happy for him. He deserves it. And I hope he has another thousand or two [hits] more."

"I don't think you can script it any better," said manager Joe Girardi. "It's movie-ready to get your 3,000th hit on a home run that ties the game and then to get 3,003 [on] a game-winner. I think we were all like, 'Wow, he really knows how to do it.'"

Still to come were the obligatory accolades from Jeter's peers, his employer and of course, from politicians.

Hall of Famer and Jeter's former Yankees teammate, Wade Boggs, welcomed Derek to the 3,000-hit club, "where he can stake his flag in the mountain and call it his own. Reaching the 3,000-hit mark is another piece of the legacy that Derek has created."

Yankees idol and Hall of Famer Yogi Berra, who finished his career with 2,150 hits: "I want to give him a big hug. It's an absolutely wonderful accomplishment."

Hal Steinbrenner, the Yankees' managing general partner, praised Jeter's "relentless team-first attitude."

New York City Mayor Michael R. Bloomberg: "New York has a greater baseball tradition than any other city, but we've never had a player get all 3,000 hits in a New York uniform until today. Congratulations, Derek. You've made all of New York City proud."

25   JETER

HE HAS BEEN IN OUR MIDST, A CONSTANT PRESENCE, FOR TWO decades, his being popping up all over the television seemingly doing one commercial endorsement after another, his countenance, a favorite among the paparazzi, splashed all over the pages of your favorite newspaper and fan magazine, his name endlessly forcing its way into the nation's gossip columns.

But what do we really know about Derek Jeter, other than what we read on the back of his bubble-gum card?

What we know for certain is that he was born in hard-to-pronounce, harder-to-spell Pequannock, New Jersey, a township in eastern Morris County some 20 miles west of the Bronx, New York, with a population of 15,540 in the 2010 census, and that he was raised in ("A, B, C, D, E, F, G, H, I got a gal in...") Kalamazoo, Michigan.

What else do we know?

We know that his mother, Dorothy, is German/Irish Catholic, and his father, Charles, is African American, the son of a single mother from Alabama.

We know that his mother and father met in Germany when they were both serving in the Army and that they nurtured Derek and his younger sister, Sharlee, with equal parts of love and discipline, imbuing them with certain values, that when their kids were little Dorothy and Charles required them to sign a commitment every August that outlined a code of behavior and comportment—study hours, curfew times, expected grades, respect for others, and no drugs or alcohol.

We know that he would like to one day be married and have children of his own (we know that because he says so, but he appears no closer now to reaching either goal than he was in 1996 when he broke in as a rookie), and we know (at least we read in the columns) that he has dated some of the most famous and most drop-dead gorgeous women in the world, a pin-up calendar–full that includes divas Mariah Carey and Joy Enriquez, Miss Universe Lara Dutta, television personality Vanessa Minillo, and actresses Jordana Brewster, Jessica Biel, and Minka Kelly.

We have seen his commercials, endorsing a wide range of products, from Ford cars and trucks to Nike, Gatorade, Fleet Bank, VISA, Discover Card, Florsheim shoes, Gillette, and Skippy peanut butter.

We are told that in 2006 he was the second-highest-paid endorser in baseball (only Ichiro Suzuki, who had the entire country of Japan in the palm of his hand, was higher), that he was ranked as the most marketable player in baseball according to the 2003, 2005, and 2010 Sports Business Surveys, and that in 2011 Nielsen ranked Jeter as the most marketable player in baseball because of his "sincerity, approachability, experience, and influence."

We have watched him play the game—even at what is normally considered an advanced age for a baseball player—with a little leaguer's mirth and joy, running full-out on every ground ball and every fly ball, mindless of the score, the inning, the opponent, or the importance of the game.

We know that he has created the Turn 2 Foundation, a charitable organization established to help children and teenagers avoid drug and alcohol addiction and to reward those with high academic achievement, and which since its inception has awarded more than $16 million in grants to youth programs in western Michigan, New York, and the Tampa Bay area.

But do we really know Derek Jeter? Does anyone?

Do we know what kind of books he likes to read (if he even reads books, that is)?

Do we know what kind of music he listens to? What kind of movies he likes? Who his favorite movies stars are (those he does not date, that is)? Which plays he has enjoyed? We have never seen a photo of him backstage at a Broadway performance, rarely even heard he has attended an opera, a concert, or a Broadway play.

Do we know what his politics are? Does he even follow politics?

Who does he vote for? Does he even vote? We never have seen a photo of him about to enter, or just emerging from, a polling booth.

What church does he attend? We don't even know if he attends church, although it is said he practices his mother's religion and there have been times he has been glimpsed making the sign of the cross as he steps into the batter's box.

Derek Jeter has been portrayed as the perfect son, the perfect friend, the perfect teammate, the perfect opponent, the perfect Yankee, the perfect representative of his trade, the "face of baseball," in the words of Commissioner Bud Selig. And no one has challenged those portrayals. In an era of rampant drug use and intense media scrutiny of professional athletes, Jeter has remained untouched by suspicion and free of scandal. He is a private person diligent in his effort to guard and protect his image. At a time when even the slightest slip is detected, Derek Jeter always says the right thing and always does the right thing. Except once.

Showing that the perfect son, the perfect friend, the perfect teammate, the perfect opponent, the perfect Yankee, the perfect representative of his trade is not perfect, Jeter's slip showed in 2011. (Isn't everyone, even a perfect one, entitled to one slip-up?)

Voted by the fans—his fans—onto the All-Star team for the 12th time and as the American League's starting shortstop for the eighth time, Jeter, citing "emotional and physical exhaustion" from his pursuit of 3,000 hits and having recently come off the disabled list because of a calf injury, chose to bypass baseball's annual mid-summer showcase event to be held in Phoenix just a few days after Jeter bagged his 3,000th hit. It was a decision uncharacteristic of Jeter, and because it was uncharacteristic it brought about an avalanche of reaction, both in defense of Jeter's decision and opposed to it. It's likely no other player would have received such a mixed reaction.

According to an anonymous official, Major League Baseball had planned to celebrate Jeter's achievement of reaching the 3,000-hit plateau and was unhappy with his decision not to attend the event.

"Derek Jeter has done everything right during his whole career," the official said. "He was wrong on this one."

According to the official, baseball would have been fine with Jeter going to Phoenix, appearing on the field during player introductions to take a bow, tipping his cap, and then leaving the stadium and heading back to New York or wherever he was planning to spend the few days off.

"This could have been a celebration of his 3,000th hit," said the baseball official. "He didn't have to play."

Yankees president Randy Levine, as expected, defended Jeter's decision and took issue with the unnamed baseball official.

"This was Derek Jeter's decision," Levine said. "He was hurt for three weeks. He felt he needed the time off. We respect that. There weren't any Major League [Baseball] officials criticizing him. If someone was criticizing him they should have the guts to not do it anonymously."

Bill Giles, Philadelphia Phillies chairman and honorary president of the National League, had the guts not to speak anonymously on the subject.

"I think it's too bad that Jeter in particular is not here because of what he accomplished over the weekend," Giles said. "I think it's a bit of a problem and baseball should study it."

Said Yankees catcher Russell Martin: "He's just coming off the DL. He played a bunch of games in a row. I'm sure the fans wanted to see him here. He just got his 3,000th hit, and the way he did it was incredible. But he's got to take care of himself and make sure that he's healthy. You have to respect that."

"I don't think it's my place to speak for others," said Cardinals outfielder Lance Berkman, who would be Jeter's teammate with the Yankees for part of the 2010 season, "but to me personally, if you get selected to be here, you have an obligation. You gotta be here. If you can go, you gotta go."

Paul Konerko, Chicago White Sox first baseman: "I think it's one thing where everyone should give him a slide, give him a break. This guy has been doing it for a long time in All-Star games, World Baseball Classic, representing the game in an awesome way, period. Maybe one time everyone should just give him a pass instead of him doing everything for everybody all the time."

Carlos Beltran: "I do believe, as a ballplayer, if you have no injuries, you should be here. The fans are the ones that vote for you and want to see you here."

Colorado Rockies shortstop Troy Tulowitzki: "Everybody would want a piece of him here [if Jeter did attend] and sometimes you need a little mental break. I'm not going to say anything bad about him because I'm probably his biggest fan."

It was left to Commissioner Bud Selig to have the final word on the subject. "Let's put the Derek Jeter question to bed," he said. "There isn't a player that I'm more proud of in the last 15 years than Derek Jeter. He has played the game like it should be played. He's even been a better human being off the field as great as he is on the field. So any concerns that I keep hearing about Derek Jeter, I know why Derek Jeter isn't here. I respect that. And I must tell you I think I would have made the same decision that Derek Jeter did.

"Derek Jeter has brought to this sport great pride. He's become a role model. Earned it. Still earning it. And so any suggestion that I, or anybody else, is unhappy with him about not being here is false."

It's because he has always done the right thing that this incident became such a tempest. Players have skipped the All-Star Game in the past with hardly a whimper of criticism. Jeter does it one time and it's a major story. Why? Because he's Derek Jeter, the perfect son, the perfect friend, the perfect teammate, the perfect opponent, the perfect Yankee, the perfect representative of his trade.

He is loyal (among his closest friends are Jorge Posada, who goes back with Jeter to 1992 and the Greensboro Hornets, and Gerald Williams, who was there when Jeter was called up to the Yankees during the 1995 season), and respectful (when the great longtime Yankees public address announcer, Bob Sheppard—the "voice of God," according to Reggie Jackson—retired, Jeter requested that the Yankees make a tape of Sheppard's introduction of Jeter coming to bat ("Now batting, number two, Derek Jeetah, number two...") and that it be played as long as Jeter remains a Yankee. He is mindful of the Yankees' legacy and of his own role in that legacy (at the old Yankee Stadium as he headed to the dugout he never failed to touch the sign in the tunnel between the clubhouse and the dugout with Joe DiMaggio's famous quote: "I want to thank the Good Lord for making me a Yankee"), and affable (he can often be seen chatting with fans as he waits in the on-deck circle, greeting the opponent's catcher playfully with a gentle tap of his bat as he steps in the batter's box, or chatting with opposing base runners who arrive at second base).

"I had a lot of animosity toward Derek Jeter early on in my career," said Chipper Jones of the Atlanta Braves, a future Hall of Famer. "He beat me in two World Series [1996 and 1999] and I didn't know him. I sat across the field from him so many times, saw all the accolades he was getting and was a little green with envy. Then I got a chance to play with him [at the 2006 World Baseball Classic]. In the clubhouse, in the dugout, off the field at dinner, this is the best dude I have ever met. This guy deserves everything."

With the media, Jeter often is evasive, noncommittal, and difficult to pin down but rarely is he aloof, assuring that he can never be accused of being uncooperative. As team captain, he understands his responsibility to be the representative of the team and to make himself available to the media, but only on a limited basis and mostly on his terms. He cooperates, but reveals little of himself, and never anything of a personal nature. He will confine his comments to matters that occur on the playing field. As sportscaster Joe Buck once said, "Derek Jeter has mastered the art of talking to the press and saying absolutely nothing."

He has limited formal education, but impeccable instincts and what is commonly known as street smarts. However you want to categorize those smarts, he's smart enough to know when to speak and what to say and when not to speak and what not to say. When, in his role as team captain, leader, and on-field representative of the Yankees, he has been called upon for public orations as he was on the final day of the old Yankee Stadium, he has demonstrated a gift for public speaking.

WHAT THEY SAY ABOUT DEREK JETER

Joe Torre: "Derek Jeter is the best player I've ever managed. I don't think there's any question. It's more than just his ability. It's his dedication to the city of New York, the New York Yankees. It's just admirable. It never stops being special to him.

"I don't think I can compare him to anybody when you consider that he may not have the most ability. I grew up in a time when

Willie Mays was special in this town and, of course, I played with Hank Aaron for eight years. But when you see what Derek has done in this town starting as a 21-year-old and still has been able to live up to himself and live up to the tradition of the Yankees, I may be biased, but he's as good as any player I've ever been around."

Robin Ventura: "I think he's the greatest Yankee of all-time. That's because of the position he plays and the era he plays in. Every play he has ever made is on tape. The players before him, nobody ever saw them fail. All we saw of them was them doing good. Every one of Derek's games has been on television. He has been criticized more than any other player in Yankee history, too; at least among the ones that were good.

"As a manager I don't like for him to come up with guys on base. I don't want him to come up when it's tied, when they need somebody on base, and I don't want him coming up late in the game to win it. He is still that kind of player."

Jesse Orosco: "You can throw him inside as much as you want, and he can still fist the ball off. You can throw the ball low and away, and he can hit with power the other way. We have pitchers' meetings and he's one of the guys where you just stay on the subject for a while. What do you do?"

Paul O'Neill: "He's the best player I've ever played with, and I think a lot of people in this clubhouse are going to say that before he's done. What sets him apart is the number of ways he can affect a game."

Reggie Jackson: "In big games, the action slows down for him where it speeds up for others. I've told him, 'I'll trade my past for your future.'"

Billy Beane: "Everything he does has such a grace about it. Maybe because of Jeter the Yankees know how to win. It's not an act. It's similar to what DiMaggio was in his era."

[Beane, the general manager of the Oakland Athletics, recalled seeing Jeter, in the prime of his career, run out a routine ground ball to shortstop in the late innings of a routine game in which the A's were beating the Yankees. Jeter made it from home to first in 4.1 seconds. It made such an impression on Beane he had his staff show videos of the play to all the players in the A's system.]

"Here you have one of the best players in the game who already had made his money and had his four championships by then and he's down three runs in the seventh inning running like that. It was a way of showing our guys, 'You think you're running hard until you see a champion and a Hall of Famer run.' It wasn't that our guys were dogging it, but this is different. If Derek Jeter can run all out all the time, everybody else better personally ask themselves why they can't."

Curt Schilling: "Derek Jeter has always been above the fray. As someone who's wallowed in it, 'foot-in-mouthed it' hundreds of times, said dumb things and backed up dumber ones, Jeter is re-freshing. He's shown up, played, and turned in a first-ballot Hall of Fame career in the hardest environment in sports to do any/all of the above. I know competing against that guy for the decade or so we matched up was what made the major leagues the major leagues for someone like me."

Chipper Jones: "When I look at him, I see a guy who's got his act together, a guy who is a winner, who does everything the right way and deserves everything he gets."

Don Zimmer: "He might go down, when it's all over, as the all-time Yankee."

Mike Trout (named to the American League All-Star team as a rookie in 2012, on being a teammate of Jeter, if only for a couple of days): "It's an honor. It's one of those things you dream about as a kid. It's pretty amazing. I'm going to try to soak in every minute and talk to him as much as I can."

Jorge Posada: "Nothing surprises me when it comes to Derek Jeter."

Andy Pettitte: "We were so young and started this run off at a young age [when the Core Four first played together as teammates with the Columbus Clippers]. Again, you knew that he was special."

Alex Rodriguez: "Fifty years from now, people are going to look at the back of [Jeter's] baseball card and see some crazy number of hits, maybe in the mid-3,000s or maybe even 4,000. But it's not going to capture half the story. For me, playing next to him I've learned so much. He's motivated me and inspired me. Derek is the ultimate grinder. He's the ultimate winner. He's like a machine. He's like a robot."

26 THE KID, THE FLIP, THE DIVE

OVER A TWO-DECADE CAREER, DEREK JETER HAS BEEN THE Captain, Mr. Clutch, and Mr. November, architect and caretaker of a career filled with an endless list of *SportsCenter* highlights. Three such highlights stand out. Known simply as the Kid, the Flip, and the Dive, they represent the magic, the instincts, and the opportunism that define Derek Jeter.

THE KID

Derek Jeter was just a rookie in 1996, a very special rookie to be sure, one who batted .314, hit 10 home runs, and drove in 78 runs during the regular season and was unanimously voted winner of the American League Rookie of the Year Award, but a rookie nonetheless.

He would bat .412 in the Division Series as the Yankees erased the Texas Rangers in four games, and now, in Yankee Stadium on the night of October 9, he was coming to bat in the bottom of the eighth inning in Game 1 of the best-of-seven American League

Championship Series against the Baltimore Orioles with the Yankees trailing 4–3.

On the mound for the Orioles was Armando Benitez, a 6'4", 200-plus-pound 23-year-old right-handed fireballer from the Dominican Republic who had been known, on occasion, to reach triple digits with his fastball. He had entered the game in the bottom of the seventh with the bases loaded and walked in a run before blowing away Mariano Duncan with fastballs to end the seventh inning.

In the bottom of the eighth, Baltimore manager Davey Johnson, opting for defense to protect his one-run lead, replaced right fielder Bobby Bonilla with Tony Tarasco. Benitez started the inning by striking out Jim Leyritz. That brought up Jeter, who already had two hits, both of them infield singles.

On the first pitch of the at-bat, Jeter, with what would become his signature "inside-out" swing, lifted a drive to right field, headed for Yankee Stadium's well-known "short porch" with Tarasco drifting back to the wall in pursuit. Here is the call of Bob Costas on NBC television:

"In right field, Tarasco going back to the track, to the wall…and what happens here? [What happens is Tarasco makes a futile plea to the umpire in right field.] He contends that a fan reaches up and touches it! But Richie Garcia says no. It's a home run! Here comes Davey Johnson, out to argue as Jeter comes across to tie the game."

Television replays and newspaper photographs show clearly that while Tarasco is reaching up to catch the ball, a young fan, who would later be identified as Jeffrey Maier, a 12-year-old Yankees fan from New Jersey who had the good sense and premonition to bring his fielder's glove to the game, is reaching over the right-field wall and, with his glove in the playing area, managed to catch Jeter's drive.

"It was like a magic trick," said Tarasco. "I was getting ready to catch it and suddenly a glove appeared and the ball disappeared.

When the kid reached over the wall, the kid's glove was very close to mine. We almost touched gloves. I was camped underneath the ball. If the ball was going out, I would've at least tried to jump. It was magic. Merlin must be in the house. Abracadabra."

After looking at replays, umpire Rich Garcia admitted he blew the call. "I don't think the ball would have gone over the fence," he said. "But I don't think he [Tarasco] would have caught it, either."

Said young Jeffrey Maier: "I didn't mean to do anything bad. I'm just a 12-year-old kid trying to catch a ball."

As would become his wont, Jeter had nothing to say on the subject, but his home run made a statement that would follow him throughout his long and spectacular career. He had come through in the clutch and tied the game. The Yankees would win it in the 11th inning on a home run by Bernie Williams and then go on to beat the Orioles, four games to one, and the Atlanta Braves, four games to two, to win their first World Series in 18 years and the first of five World Series championships in the era of the Core Four.

THE FLIP

It was the play that would come to define Derek Jeter, the play that would prompt Bernie Williams to say of his teammate, "When you see that, you appreciate how great a player he is," and Ron Washington to comment, "That's why Derek Jeter is Derek Jeter."

It came on Saturday, October 13, 2001, in Oakland, and it was so unexpected, so startling, so inspired, that it not only defied belief, it became a part of the Jeter legacy and the Jeter mystique. It was a play that we came to believe, because of his uncanny instincts and his knack for being in the right place at the right time, only Derek Jeter could have made.

The Yankees had dominated the American League East, winning 95 games and losing 65 and finishing 13½ games ahead of the Boston Red Sox. But the Oakland Athletics, although finishing 14 games behind the Seattle Mariners in the American League East, had won 102 games and would be a formidable foe for the Yankees in the Division Series.

Things looked bleak for the Yankees when Mark Mulder beat Roger Clemens in Game 1 and Tim Hudson out-pitched Andy Pettitte in Game 2, both games in Yankee Stadium. No team had ever lost the first two games at home and come back to win a five-game playoff series.

Game 3 was another pitcher's duel of 17-game winners, Mike Mussina for the Yankees, Barry Zito for the Athletics. As they went to the bottom of the seventh inning, both pitchers had allowed just two hits, but because one of the Yankees' two hits was a fifth-inning home run by Jorge Posada, Mussina and the Yankees had the upper hand and a 1–0 lead.

In the bottom of the seventh, Mussina quickly disposed of Jermaine Dye on a pop-fly to shortstop and Eric Chavez on a fly ball to center field. But Jeremy Giambi, Jason's younger brother, smacked a single to right to bring up Terrence Long, a 25-year-old left-handed hitter from Montgomery, Alabama, who had batted .288 and .283 in two seasons with the Athletics with 18 and 12 home runs, and 80 and 85 runs batted in.

Long whistled a line drive into the right-field corner that sent Giambi spinning around the bases. He was rounding third base when right fielder Shane Spencer retrieved the ball and fired home. But Spencer's throw sailed over the cut-off man, first baseman Tino Martinez, and bounced down the first base line, an errant throw that surely would score Giambi with the tying run.

Seemingly out of nowhere, and out of position, there was Derek Jeter. Seeing that the throw was off-line and was going to miss the cut-off man, Jeter made a beeline across the field from his shortstop position to retrieve the ball in foul territory between first base and home plate. In one motion and with not a moment to spare he caught the ball and flipped it backhanded to home plate, where catcher Jorge Posada grabbed it and applied the tag on Giambi, who tried to score standing up. If he had slid, he probably would have been safe. Jeter's flip was right on the money, up the line slightly toward third base to Posada's left— the perfect spot for him to grab it and tag the runner without a wasted motion. If Jeter's throw was to Posada's right, there is no way he would have time to grab it and tag the runner before he reached home plate.

Jeter never should have been there. He should have been covering second base for a possible play on Long, the go-ahead run. Why was he there?

There was no answer. As suggested by Ron Washington, the then-third-base coach for Oakland, who is now the manager of the Texas Rangers, it was merely Jeter being Jeter, acting on instinct, being in the right place at the right time.

"Derek Jeter noticed that there was nobody over there to back it up and he left where he should have been and went over there and did what he did," Washington said. "It was Derek Jeter that made that play. If Derek doesn't touch that ball, he's safe. No doubt about it.

"That's what you call awareness on the ballfield. He was definitely not supposed to be there. I wish he wouldn't have been there. That's Derek Jeter, man. That's why he's a champion."

The Yankees won the game 1–0. They won Game 4 by a score of 9–2. And back home in Yankee Stadium for Game 5, they won 5–3, and advanced to the World Series.

THE DIVE

There was no pennant on the line in Yankee Stadium on the night of Thursday July 1, 2004, the Yankees holding a commanding and seemingly uncatchable 7½ game lead in the American League East. It was not a must-win situation in Yankee Stadium, but it was the

Yankees against the Red Sox, the consummate rivalry, and that alone made it special.

They had battled for almost four hours, through 11 tension-packed innings, the Yankees jumping out to a 2–0 run lead in the second on a walk to Jorge Posada and a home run by Tony Clark off Pedro Martinez, and adding a run in the fifth on Posada's home run. The Red Sox fought back with two in the sixth on Manny Ramirez's two-run homer, followed by one run in the seventh.

Now it was the top of the 12th, with the score still tied 3–3, two outs and Red Sox runners on second and third when Trot Nixon lifted a high, twisting pop-fly near the seats in short left field and Derek Jeter in reckless and determined pursuit.

We never did learn if the ball, had it dropped, would have been fair or foul, but in the next few moments we would witness another addition to the Jeter legacy, another example of his competitiveness and his willingness to put his body in harm's way, all for the ultimate goal of winning a game. Traveling at break-neck speed, and with utter disregard for his own safety, Jeter caught up with the ball either just barely before the foul line or just barely after it, snared it, and then, unable to halt his momentum or avoid the inevitable, went flying headfirst into the seats. He would emerge moments later with the baseball still in his glove and blood pouring from a cut over his right eye, fortunate to have avoided serious injury.

Jeter left the game, which the Yankees would win an inning later on a pinch-hit RBI single by John Flaherty, and was taken to nearby Columbia Presbyterian Hospital, where seven stitches were taken to close the gash on his right cheek. He was back in the starting lineup the following night for an interleague game against the New York Mets in Shea Stadium.

Blessed with good genes, good health, and good fortune, in the 15-year period from 1996 to 2010, Jeter has appeared in more games than any other player in the major leagues, a total of 2,280 of the Yankees 2,428 games, a remarkable 94 percent of his team's games.

DIMAG AND "D" CAPTAIN

Babe Ruth, Lou Gehrig, Joe DiMaggio, Mickey Mantle, Yogi Berra, Whitey Ford, Reggie Jackson. And Derek Jeter?

The mind boggles. The imagination trembles. The idea astounds.

Who would have thought that this Michigan kid, this 21st-century interloper, would take his place alongside the greatest names of sport's greatest team, and deservedly so; that this erstwhile skinny shortstop would be aligned with the gods of the game whose legacy go as far back as 100 years; that he would topple records and achieve heights that never were attained by any of them.

Where does Derek Jeter rank in this pantheon? Is he the greatest of all New York Yankees? One of the three greatest?

Of that Mount Rushmore of Yankees, the one Derek Jeter most closely resembles in style and substance is Joe DiMaggio, the Yankee Clipper. Jeter does not have the power game of a Ruth, a Gehrig, a Mantle, or a Jackson, but he has the grace and the elegance of a DiMaggio, and at the risk of being accused of heresy, he even out-DiMaggios DiMaggio.

To be sure, Joe D. deserves his props. He played only 13 seasons (Jeter has played 18 seasons), having lost three prime years to military service during World War II, his career cut short by a debilitating bone spur on his foot.

Jeter never has come close to DiMaggio's incredible, probably unbreakable, record of hitting in 56 straight games, which has lasted more than 70 years, or to matching Joe's career mark of only 369 strikeouts, a miniscule 13 of them in the 1941 season.

But DiMaggio never came close to 3,000 hits and had only two seasons of 200 hits or more (Jeter has eight). DiMaggio never stole as many as 10 bases in a season, Jeter has done it 16 times and has eight seasons of 20 or more steals.

DiMaggio batted .271 in 10 World Series. Jeter has batted .321 in seven World Series.

Carrying the DiMaggio/Jeter comparison (debate?) further:

In his first six seasons (1936–41) DiMaggio's Yankees won 598 games (99.7 per year in a 154-game schedule) and failed to win the World Series only once.

In his first five full seasons (1996–00) Jeter's Yankees won 487 games (97.4 per year in a 162-game schedule) and failed to win the World Series only once.

In his first five seasons, including the regular season and the World Series, DiMaggio scored 625 runs, had 994 hits, and played in 19 World Series games with a record of 16–3.

In his first five full seasons, including the regular season and the World Series, Jeter scored 619 runs, had 1,022 hits, and played in 19 World Series games with a record of 16–3.

27 ANDY RETURNS...AGAIN

*"You spend a good piece of your life gripping a
baseball and in the end it turns out that it
was the other way around all the time."*

— Jim Bouton

HE HAD BEEN GRIPPING THE BASEBALL FOR MORE THAN TWO-
thirds of his life, and now, when he should have joined the pipe-
and-slippers set, he couldn't let go, and so the on-again, off-again,
in-again, out-again Andy Pettitte soap opera was on again.

Would he be making a comeback? Again?

Pettitte thought it was over for him. He *really* did when on
February 4, 2011, at a gala press conference at Yankee Stadium
jam-packed with Yankees brass and employees, members of the
print and electronic media, still photographers, television camera-
men, and assorted friends, relatives, and hangers-on, he announced
his retirement.

"I am not going to play this season," he had said on February
4, 2011. "I can tell you that 100 percent. But I guess you can never
say never."

And now, 406 days later, on March 16, 2012, three months before his 40th birthday, the Yankees announced that Andy Pettitte
was coming back. Again.

The news created a buzz in the Yankees' training camp—all of it good. His teammates, the older ones and the younger ones, were excited that Andy was coming back. Not because the team needed him, but because the players wanted him for who he is, respected and loved, not just for what he could do.

Alex Rodriguez called Pettitte "a road map that people can follow. What he brings is priceless. It is beyond what he does when he pitches."

"He'll add to our team on the field and off the field," said Derek Jeter. "I would assume everyone's excited."

This latest comeback had its roots three months earlier, when Pettitte heard that Yankees general manager Brian Cashman said he would welcome a comeback from the veteran left-hander. Pettitte, who had stayed active at home by throwing batting practice to his two sons, began throwing in earnest and reached out to Cashman to give him a progress report.

At one point, Cashman made Pettitte an offer. He could come back to the Yankees on a one-year contract for a salary in the $10-to-$12-million range, but Pettitte said he was not ready to make such a commitment. A few weeks later, Cashman swung two deals to acquire two pitchers, veteran right-hander Hiroki Kuroda as a free agent and young right-hander Michael Pineda in a trade with the Seattle Mariners.

With the Yankees now well-stocked with pitchers and their budget stretched to the max, the deals seemed to put an end to a Pettitte re-signing. There remained a small opening, however. Pettitte was to attend spring training in Tampa as a guest instructor (it has long been the Yankees' wont to invite their retired stars to spring training to serve as window dressing) and he asked Cashman for permission to pitch the occasional batting practice. Permission granted.

One day in Tampa, Pettitte cornered Cashman and told the GM that he had the old urge back, he was throwing and he would like an opportunity to give a comeback a try. Cashman agreed and arranged for Pettitte to throw a clandestine bullpen session in order to determine if he still had his good stuff after a year layoff. And so, in the wee hours of the morning, approximately 7:30 AM, on March 13, in the presence of Cashman, manager Joe Girardi, pitching coach Larry Rothschild, and special assistant GM Gene Michael, Pettitte had his audition and received unanimous approval in the form of a thumbs up from the panel of experts.

"Once I stood on that mound the other morning, it was like I'd never left," Pettitte said. "Even though it was Tuesday morning, Cashman was standing there with Gene Michael, Joe [Girardi] and Larry [Rothschild]. It was just like I had never left. It was weird."

Cashman got permission from Hal Steinbrenner, the Yankees managing general partner, to stretch the budget slightly and offer Pettitte a contract, but he had to tell Andy that instead of the $10 to $12 million he had offered earlier, the best he could do was one-year at $2.5 million.

"He's worth more than that if he's right," Cashman said. "There is no downside. This guy knows how to pitch even when his stuff is not great. As long as he's healthy, he's in position to help us."

"For what I'm coming back and playing for, it's an awful lot of money and I realize that," Pettitte said. "It's a long ways from what we were talking about in January. I've just got to follow what I feel like my heart is telling me to do. I have a desire to work again. As a man, I want to go to work and my work is baseball and it's pitching. That's what I know, so I'm going to try to get it cranked back up and do it again."

Coincidentally, at the time the Yankees were having concerns about one of their two newest arms, Pineda, whose velocity had dwindled from a reported high of the upper 90s to the lower 90s (he would be placed on the disabled list with tendinitis on March 31 and eventually have surgery on May 1 for a tear of the interior labrum in his right shoulder), so the Yankees would be in the market for a pitcher anyway. But even if they weren't, they'd still be interested.

"This is Andy Pettitte," Cashman said. "How do you say no to that potential asset, despite what you have? All that equipment is still there, or should still be there. Let's go see. Why not? Does it complicate things? Yeah it does, but Andy Pettitte's worth complicating things for."

If not for the money, why was Pettitte coming back?

"This is all about me having the desire to do this again," he said. "I really believe that mentally I'll be able to get back to where I was. I believe that if I'm mentally right, I'm going to win. I just believe that. For me it's a no-brainer. I'm not scared. I don't think I'm going to fail, but I'm not scared to come back. I'm not worried about that. I'm going to trust that I know in my heart I'm doing the right thing. And I'm hoping and praying that it's going to be great."

Pettitte was reminded that at his press conference in Yankee Stadium in 2011 he said he would be embarrassed if he was forced to change his mind and unretire.

"I am embarrassed that I'm coming back," he admitted. "But then I'm like, 'What can I do?' Things have changed. My desire to do this has changed and I sure as heck don't want to look back [in] 10 years and say, 'Man, I wish I would have done that.'"

Pettitte would spend the next two months getting in playing shape, building up his arm strength, facing live hitters in minor league games, all with the intention of being ready to pitch for the Yankees by mid-May.

In 2004, when Pettitte became a free agent, left the Yankees, and signed with the Houston Astros, Roger Clemens also became a free agent, left the Yankees, and followed Pettitte to Houston.

Three years later Pettitte became a free agent a second time and returned to the Yankees. Five months later Clemens, who had announced his retirement after the 2006 season, came out of retirement and returned to the Yankees as a free agent in '07.

Pettitte and Clemens were best friends. They were as close as brothers.

But now, on May 1, 2012 (coincidentally the same day Michael Pineda was undergoing surgery), Pettitte was in Washington, D.C., having been called as a witness in the U.S. government's perjury case against his former friend.

Under oath, and with Clemens present (Pettitte never looked at Clemens, never acknowledged him; Clemens never acknowledged Pettitte and the two never spoke), Pettitte said that some years earlier, either 1999 or 2000, Clemens told him he had taken human growth hormone.

"We were working out at Roger's house in the gym," Pettitte said. "Roger had mentioned to me that he had taken HGH and that it could help with recovery. That's really all I remember about the conversation."

When he was on the stand, Clemens denied ever telling Pettitte he used HGH, commenting that Andy must have "misremembered." Under cross examination from Clemens' defense attorney, Pettitte backed off his statement that Roger told him he had used HGH. Clemens was acquitted of the charge of perjury, but the rift between Clemens and Pettitte had not been repaired.

Pettitte's comeback debut came in Yankee Stadium against the Seattle Mariners on May 13. He pitched 6⅓ innings, allowed four runs—all earned—seven hits, walked three, and struck out two as he was tagged with the loss in a 6–2 defeat. He wasn't great, but he wasn't terrible, either. It was a start.

Five days later, in an interleague game against the Cincinnati Reds, he was the Andy Pettitte of old, the familiar icy stare from behind the glove that practically covered his face all the way up to his emotionless eyes, the impassive visage, the steely gaze as he baffled hitters for eight tantalizing shutout innings. He allowed four hits, walked one, and struck out nine in a 4–0 victory, the first win of his comeback, the 241st win of his major league career, 204 of them as a Yankee. He would win two of his next three starts, including 7⅓ shutout innings, two hits, two walks, and 10 strikeouts in a 7–0 victory over the Tampa Bay Rays on June 5.

Pettitte pitched decently in his next three starts, but failed to win a game. Then, in the fifth inning of a June 27 game in Cleveland, he was struck on the left leg by a line drive off the bat of Casey Kotchman and suffered a broken fibula (just above the ankle). Pettitte would try to accelerate his rehab and suffer a setback that would sideline him for 11 weeks, an eternity for a 40-year-old pitcher.

Pettitte returned on September 19 against the Toronto Blue Jays, pitched five shutout innings (four hits, two walks, three strikeouts) and picked up the win in the Yankees' 4–2 victory. Five days later against the Twins in Minnesota, he pitched six shutout innings (seven hits, one walk, three strikeouts) and was the winning pitcher in a 5–3 victory.

Through 2012, Pettitte had won 208 games as a Yankee, placing him third on their all-time list to Whitey Ford and Red Ruffing. Again, it's not too great a leap of faith to project that, had he won the same number of games (37) for the Yankees that he won in his three years with the Astros, he would stand at 243 for his Yankees' career, or 12 more than Ruffing and nine more than Ford.

The question for the ages, and for future Hall of Fame voters, will be whether Pettitte has the qualifications to warrant admittance in Cooperstown.

His 245 regular season wins with the Yankees and Astros (51st on the all-time list, one behind "Iron Man" Joe McGinnity and Amos Rusie), .633 winning percentage (44th on the all-time list, .0050 behind Jim Palmer), 3.86 earned run average, 3,130⅔ innings, and 2,320 strikeouts (44th all-time, 14 behind Early Wynn, 37 behind Robin Roberts, 76 behind Sandy Koufax), plus his all-time-best 19 postseason wins, make him a borderline Hall of Famer. Not a shoo-in by any means, but certainly in the conversation.

Unfortunately, by his own admission, those numbers are tainted, and they likely will keep a large segment of the voting members of the Baseball Writers Association of America from voting for Pettitte when he becomes Hall of Fame eligible,

Consequently, rather than possibly spending his retirement years basking in Hall of Fame glory, Pettitte is likely to spend them in performance-enhancement-drug infamy.

28 FALSE STEP

THEIR GLASSES HALF EMPTY, THE GLOOM AND DOOMERS SAW IT as a bad omen.

Opening day of the 2012 baseball season, the Tampa Bay Rays hosting the New York Yankees at Tropicana Field in sunny St. Petersburg, the Yankees rallied from a four-run first inning eruption by the Rays to come from behind with two runs in the second and four in the third. Now, leading 6–5 going into the bottom of the ninth, it was time for manager Joe Girardi to call on his closer, the invincible one, Mariano Rivera.

What happened next was unthinkable, unlikely, unbelievable, and unsettling.

On a 1–2 pitch, Desmond Jennings singled up the middle to lead off the inning.

Ben Zobrist hit Rivera's next pitch into the right-center gap for a triple. Jennings scored the tying run.

Evan Longoria was walked intentionally.

Luke Scott was walked intentionally to load the bases.

In a standard, time-tested move, Yankees manager Joe Girardi brought his infield and his outfield in to try to cut the winning run off at home plate.

Sean Rodriguez struck out.

Carlos Pena sent a fly ball to left center that sailed over the heads of left fielder Brett Gardner and center fielder Curtis Granderson, and Zobrist scored easily with the winning run.

It was the first game of the season, only 161 games remaining. No reason to panic, but…Mariano Rivera, the peerless closer, had blown a save!

He had suffered a loss!

His earned run average was 54.00!

He was 42 years old!

Did doubt creep into the hearts and minds of Yankees fans? Maybe a little. Maybe more than a little.

Three days later in Baltimore, Rivera was brought in to pitch again in the ninth inning with the Yankees leading 6–2. It was not a save situation, but it was a significant early-season game because the Yankees had been swept in three games by the Rays and because it could reveal something about their closer.

This time Rivera was on his game. He allowed a one-out double to Robert Andino, but otherwise escaped unscathed.

Over the next 21 days, Rivera would pitch seven more times with his usual superlative results. On April 30, again against the Orioles, but this time in Yankee Stadium, Rivera entered in the ninth inning with the Yankees leading 2–1. He retired Nolan Reimold on an easy ground ball to second, gave up a solid single to center to J.J. Hardy, and then got Nick Markakis to hit a soft ground ball to shortstop that Derek Jeter turned into a double play, eliciting from Yankees radio broadcaster John Sterling his familiar cry of "Duh Yankees win….DUHHHH YANKEEES WINNNNNN!"

Since his Opening Day loss, Rivera made eight appearances with the following results: eight innings, no runs, three hits, seven strikeouts, no walks, one win, and five saves. His earned-run average dropped from 54.00 to 2.16. The Yankees, winners of 13 of their last 19 games, were 13–9, a game and a half behind Tampa Bay.

The surprising Orioles won the next two games in Yankee Stadium. On Tuesday night, May 1, they beat the Yankees 7–1 as Chris Davis and J.J. Hardy torched Phil Hughes with home runs. On the getaway game, Wednesday night, May 2, Jake Arrieta pitched eight shutout innings, allowing five hits and striking out nine and the Orioles hit two more home runs to beat Ivan Nova 5–0. The loss dropped the Yankees to 13–11 and into fourth place in the American League East, 3½ games behind the Tampa Bay Rays, 2½ games behind the Orioles and a half game behind the Toronto Blue Jays.

After the game, the Yankees boarded a charter plane for the flight to Kansas City, where they would begin a four-game series against the Royals the following night.

Early on the evening of Thursday, May 3, Mariano Rivera, dressed in his spiked baseball shoes and baseball pants and a dark gray short-sleeved zippered pullover with the words "New York" emblazoned along the chest, and jogged out to center field of Kansas City's Kauffman Stadium during batting practice to shag fly balls.

Those who said Rivera was tempting fate by shagging fly balls were obviously unaware that it was something he had done a few thousand times, almost every day or night since he became a professional baseball player 22 years earlier, without being injured. He had not been on the disabled list in nine years.

Rivera enjoyed shagging fly balls. It was good exercise, good for keeping his legs in shape, and it was fun. And he was good at it. With his agile, lithe, and supple athletic body that belied his 42 years, Rivera was so graceful and so skilled at running down those fly balls, more than a few of his managers and teammates said that if he chose to, he could have made it as in the major leagues as an outfielder. One of his minor league managers said Mariano was "the best center fielder on this team."

It was slightly after 6:00 PM Central Daylight Time when Jayson Nix hit a batting-practice fastball to the deepest part of center field

where Rivera, following the flight of the ball, took off in his languid, loping gait. Man and ball reached the fence at approximately
the same time and the man leaped to snare the ball as it was about
to hit the wall. Instead, Rivera's knee appeared to collapse under
his weight. Rivera fell to the ground on the center-field warning
track, grabbing his right leg as he writhed in obvious pain.

"Oh my God," said Alex Rodriguez waiting his turn in the batting cage some 400 feet away.

Concerned Yankees gathered around Rivera, curious to see
how badly their fallen teammate, friend, idol, and meal ticket was
hurt and seeking to comfort him.

Seeing his star closer writhing on the ground, manager Joe
Girardi, accompanied by bullpen coach Mike Harkey and head
trainer Steve Donohue, rushed to Rivera's aid. They carefully
helped Rivera get to his feet and gently placed him in a golf cart
that had arrived quickly on the scene. Rivera had a slight smile on
his face as the cart transported him to the Yankees' dugout, where
he spoke briefly with solicitous teammates before being taken to
an opening in the right-field wall that led to the street. As he departed, the smile had left his face and had been replaced by the
grim look of concern, worry, and fear for the worst.

Rivera was taken to nearby Kansas University MedWest
Hospital, where an MRI revealed a torn ACL and a torn meniscus
of the right knee.

"That's about as bad as it gets," Girardi said. "You lose a Hall of
Famer, it changes a lot. We like the depth of our bullpen and it just
got a little bit shorter. We'll have to find a way to get through it."

The next night Rivera showed up in the Yankees clubhouse
walking with the aid of crutches and wearing a bandage on his
right knee and an occasional smile on his face. He was in relatively good spirits as he talked about his injury and the future. The
night before he gloomily said he didn't know if he would ever play
again, but 24 hours later he was singing a different tune.

All spring there had been speculation whether the 2012 season would be Rivera's last. It was the final year of his contract and although he refused to be drawn into a discussion regarding a new contract, neither would he admit that 2012 would be his swan song.

If he had made a decision about his future, he kept it to himself. He dropped enough hints that led to the conclusion that he would go out after the season in a blaze of glory and get on with his life, spend more time with his wife and three boys, concentrate on running the Mariano Rivera Foundation—which distributes more than $500,000 to underprivileged children in the United States and Panama—provide Christmas gifts to children, develop a program that provides computer access and adult mentors to children, resume building an elementary school and church in his native Panama, and contemplate the possibility of entering the ministry.

But now his injury had apparently caused a change of heart.

"I'm coming back," he declared. "Write it down in big letters. I'm not going out like this. When you love the game and you like to compete, it would be tough to go out like this. I love to play the game. To me, going out like this isn't the right way. I don't think like that. With the strength of the Lord, I have to continue."

Someone asked, facetiously no doubt, if the Yankees would want him back.

Rivera laughed.

"Oh, yeah," he said. "They will want the old goat."

This news, after the gloom of the night before, to a man lifted the spirit of the Yankees.

"I've never seen a clubhouse so depressed," said Rodriguez. "It's great to hear he'll be back. I love the man. But it's surprising. I thought it was over this year, but I guess Mo is all about endings and he wants to end it the right way."

"I was thinking he was coming back anyway," said Mark Teixeira. "I didn't believe he was going to retire. He is still one of the best players in the game. It's great to hear [that Rivera will be coming back] and it will be good for his rehab, something for him to look forward to."

"Everyone is happy to hear that," said the Captain, Derek Jeter, "but we can't sit around and wait. Injuries are unfortunate. Injuries happen. But we still have work to do and jobs to do. We can't count the days."

Rivera promised to be around the team as much as possible during his rehab, to lend a hand in any way he could, even if only as a cheerleader.

"I always put myself last," he said. "I'm a positive man. I'm okay. The only thing is that I feel sorry that I let down my teammates. But besides that, I'm okay. And the team will be okay, too.

"I'll be around. We will talk. All my advice and all my knowledge will be there. I'm just going to give them encouragement that I trust them and believe in them. They can do the job. They will do the job."

True to his word, Rivera showed up frequently at Yankee Stadium, offered his encouragement, his advice, his support, served as a mentor, and cheered for his teammates. Into the breach came the veteran Rafael Soriano, who did a tremendous job as the Yankees closer. He was everything the Yankees hoped he would be, wanted him to be, needed him to be.

He just wasn't Mariano Rivera.

29 REBOUND

ALL OF A SUDDEN, DEREK JETER WAS ALONE, THE ONLY MEMBER of the Yankees' Core Four in the clubhouse, on the charter airplane to away games; the only one still pulling on a uniform every day.

Jorge Posada, "Sado," his closest friend on the team, the one who frequently accompanied him on his drive to and from Yankee Stadium, had vanished into retirement at the end of the previous season.

Mariano Rivera, "Mo," the dependable solid rock of the team's bullpen, their indispensable weapon, was walking on crutches, awaiting surgery, finished for this year, at least.

Andy Pettitte, "Handy Andy," the steady one who had left and come back, left again and come back again, was missing once more, in Tampa rehabbing a broken fibula.

Now only Derek Jeter remained.

As the 2012 major league baseball season opened, Jeter was only 12 weeks away from his 38th birthday, an age when logic, history, and medical science dictate that a professional athlete is in decline. Except for a receding hairline, Derek Jeter didn't look his age. He still was trim—not the skinny rookie of 1996, but no heavier than the World Series Most Valuable Player of 2000—and he still played with a little boy's joy and an athlete's grace and fluidity.

At bat, he looked the same as always, striding into the batter's box, tugging at his helmet and raising his right hand to the home plate umpire as if to say, "I'm not ready; I'll let you know when I am," a gesture that has become a standard ritual of young baseball players in New York, New Jersey, and Connecticut, in fact, throughout the nation. (Go to a Little League, high school, even a college baseball game and notice how many young hitters will stride into the batter's box and raise their back hand to the home plate umpire as if to say, "I'm not ready; I'll let you know when I am.")

Jeter still held his bat high above his right ear, still had the quick hands, still had the ability to take an inside pitch and with his familiar inside-out swing hit a line drive inside the right-field foul line.

Jeter began the season with 3,088 hits, 20th on baseball's all-time hit list.

On April 20, in a 6–2 win over the Red Sox in Boston, he passed his childhood idol, Dave Winfield, for 19th place.

On May 13, the Yankees lost to the Mariners 6–2, and Jeter passed Tony Gwynn for 18th place. The next day, in Baltimore, he passed Robin Yount for 17th place.

The Yankees were off to their familiar slow start, a record of 22–21, 5½ games out of first place on May 22.

Five days later, Jeter passed Paul Waner for 16th place on the all-time hit list.

A day after that, he passed George Brett for 15th place as the Yankees began their comeback with their fifth straight win, a 2–0 shutout of the Athletics in Oakland.

On June 12, the Yankees beat the Braves 6–4 in Atlanta and moved into first place in the American League East.

On June 26, his 38th birthday, in a 6–4 win against the Cleveland Indians, Jeter slammed out two more hits, giving him 3,183 for his career. On his 38th birthday the all-time hit leader Pete Rose had 3,170 hits.

Three days later, while the Yankees were being blown out 14–7 by the White Sox in Chicago, Jeter had one hit in four at-bats, a double, and passed Cal Ripken Jr. for 14th place on the all-time hit list.

The Yankees would win 35 out of 48 games and open a commanding 10-game lead in the AL East on July 18.

On August 14, the Yankees were in a slight decline, their AL East lead shaved to six games by the charge of the surprising Baltimore Orioles. Hideki Kuroda stopped the bleeding with a complete game, two-hit, 3–0 victory over the Texas Rangers at Yankee Stadium. Jeter had a pair of singles and moved into 13th place on baseball's all-time hit list ahead of Nap Lajoie.

The Yankees' decline, and the Orioles' surge, continued through the month of August, while on August 21, Jeter moved past Eddie Murray into 12th place on the all-time hit list.

On Tuesday September 4, the Yankees were beaten by the Tampa Bay Rays 5–2, while the Orioles were slaughtering the Toronto Blue Jays 12–0, wiping out the Yankees' entire 10-game lead. The Yanks and O's were now in an exact tie for first place and the Rays were only 1½ games back.

For the next 19 days, the Yankees and Orioles would be separated by no more than one game, but the Orioles never could pass the Yanks in the standing, except for a few hours on September 14 when the Yankees lost to Tampa Bay at Yankee Stadium. A couple of hours later, the Orioles lost to the Athletics in Oakland, and the deadlock for first place in the AL East remained.

In the Yankees defeat, Jeter had two more hits, pushing his career total to 3,285 and moving him into 11th place all-time, ahead of the "Say Hey Kid," the incomparable Willie Mays, voted baseball's greatest living player.

When he learned Jeter had passed him, Mays was gracious and lavish in his praise of the Yankees' shortstop, whom he had met briefly at an All-Star game and who was born eight months after Mays played his last game.

"What I noticed is that he is a very, very nice person, not just the ballplayer," said Mays, 43 years Jeter's senior. "He's a good person and that's what really comes across when you meet him. He puts his team first, that's the way I played the game. There are some guys who don't do that. Derek knows how to play the game. He makes the players around him better."

A ROSE IS A ROSE IS A....

Don't call Pete Rose egotistical, even though he does have an ego—a large one.

Don't call Pete Rose arrogant, even though he has a high opinion of his place in baseball history.

Don't call Pete Rose envious, even though he is protective of his record 4,256 hits.

What you can call Pete Rose is a baseball pragmatist and a records realist.

In assessing Derek Jeter and his chances of catching and passing the all-time hit record, Rose, in an exclusive interview with journalist Joe Posnanski, was complimentary but analytical as he addressed the possibility of Jeter breaking his record with logic, statistics, and probabilities.

"I like Jeter," Rose emphasized. "I admire him. What's not to like? He comes to the ballpark and busts his hump every day. He gets his uniform dirty. Do you ever see Derek Jeter not run out a ground ball?"

But break the hit record? That's another story.

"What does he have now? What, 3,303 hits? (Actually, 3,304. Rose had failed to include a hit in Jeter's last game of the 2012 season.)

"I don't think he will break the record. First of all, I don't think he wants to leave the Yankees. (Rose left the Cincinnati Reds and played five years with the Philadelphia Phillies and one with the Montreal Expos before returning to the Reds.) And the Yankees, they're about winning. Jeter had a great year this year, but he's what? Thirty-eight years old? And he's a shortstop? How many 40-year-old shortstops you see walking around? Not too many, right? And they can't put him at third base because A-Rod's there. They can't put him at second base 'cause Cano's there. He don't help them in left field—he's got to be in the center of things, you know what I mean? What are they going to do? Put him at first base?"

Sounding more like an actuary or a member in good standing of SABR (Society for American Baseball Research) than a former ballplayer with the numbers seemingly at his fingertips or etched indelibly in his mind, Rose continued:

"He still needs 950 (actually 952) hits, right? He had a great year this year, but you think he can do that again? At 39? A shortstop? Let's say he does it again. Let's say he gets 200 more hits next year. And let's say he gets 200 more hits when he's 40, though I don't think he can. Okay, can he get 200 more hits when he's 41? You think he can?

"I don't think he can get 200 more hits at 41, but let's say he does. Okay, now he's 42. He's going to get 200 more hits then? At 42? Let me tell you, I've been there, the body locks up. Jeter's a great hitter. I'd say he hits like I did. But he's gonna get 200 hits when he's 42? I don't think he will. And even if he does all that, he's still 150 hits short.

"I'd say Jeter will probably end up in batting average about where I was. We're about the same—me, Derek, Hank [Aaron],

Willie [Mays]. We were all hitting about .311 or .312 or .313 when we got into our late thirties, maybe Willie was a little lower [through their age-38 season, Jeter was hitting .313, Rose .312, Aaron .311, Mays .307], and we all ended up around .303 or .305 [Aaron .305, Rose .303, Mays .302]. Jeter will probably end up where I did, right around there. So if his average is around the same as mine, he has to get about as many at-bats as I did. I got 14,053 at-bats. What's he got? Ten thousand? Eleven thousand? [Through the 2012 season, Jeter had 10,551 at-bats.] He's a great hitter. How's he going to get 3,500 more at-bats? I think time's running out."

Informed of Rose's comments, Jeter as usual refused to be drawn into any kind of controversy and seemed to be amused, but baffled, by the subject.

"Why would you think about something that's 1,000 hits away?" Jeter replied. "I don't think about that, really. That's the least of my concerns right now is the best way to put it. I didn't think about 3,000 hits. I'm trying to win, that's it. You do it long enough, I guess, good things happen. But I'm not thinking about that.

"It's hard to get 3,000 hits. You have to get 200 hits for 15 years, man. That's a lot of hits. Four thousand is 20 years of it so, really, I don't know why we're talking about it. Can I catch him today? Then it's not a story."

Jeter did admit that there is one record on his mind—and it's not Rose's.

"The only one I'm thinking about catching is Yogi [Berra, who has earned 10 World Series–championship rings]. I always tell Yogi he's really only got five because they went straight to the World Series. [In Berra's day there was no division playoff, no league championship series, and no wild-card; to reach the World Series you merely finished first in the eight- or ten-team American League or National League.) I always cut it in half. He just laughs."

The Yankees didn't shake loose of the overachieving Orioles until the final day of the season, officially clinching the division title when the Orioles lost to the Tampa Bay Rays. A short time later the Yankees finished off a 14–2 victory over the Red Sox as Curtis Granderson and Robinson Cano both hit a pair of home runs, Granderson finishing the regular season with 43 home runs—one behind the league leader, Miguel Cabrera of the Detroit Tigers—and 106 RBI. Cano finished with 33 homers and 94 RBI.

Rafael Soriano more than filled in adequately for the indispensable Mariano Rivera with 42 saves, third in the league. Kuroda and Phil Hughes each won 16 games and CC Sabathia won 15.

And Derek Jeter, 38 years old, was Derek Jeter.

Jeter was a .300 hitter for the 12th time in his career, his .316 good for fifth place in the American League.

Jeter led the league in hits with 216 and no other shortstop in the history of baseball—not Honus Wagner, not Cal Ripken Jr., not Omar Vizquel, ever got 200 hits at age 38.

Jeter led the league in plate appearances for the fifth time in his career with 740. Nobody else ever led the league in plate appearances at age 38, not Pete Rose and not Methuselah.

"That's not supposed to happen unless you're maybe a DH," said a reflective, admiring Joe Girardi. "He played shortstop every day and he played hurt. It's truly remarkable. It's one of the greatest seasons I've ever seen, considering all the factors."

At age 38, Jeter started 158 of the Yankees 162 games, 133 at shortstop, 25 as the designated hitter, and he still wasn't finished for the year.

"The fact that he was able to get so many at-bats and stay out there every day exceeded my expectations," Girardi said. "I talked about wanting to get him days off. I DHed him sometimes but I had to play him more in the field than I probably wanted to just because of some of the [injuries] we were going through."

Derek Jeter was going to have to get used to hearing the name Pete Rose, reading it alongside his own name, answering questions that would include that name. He was destined to be compared with him, chasing him, surpassing him for the remainder of his career, however long that would be.

In the 2012 season, Jeter had passed Dave Winfield, Tony Gwynn, Robin Yount, Paul Waner, George Brett, Cal Ripken Jr., Nap Lajoie, Eddie Murray, and Willie Mays.

Still ahead of him—the *only* ones ahead of him—were Eddie Collins, Paul Molitor, Carl Yastrzemski, Honus Wagner, Cap Anson (who got his last hit 115 years ago), Tris Speaker, Stan Musial, Henry Aaron, Ty Cobb, and Pete Rose.

The mind boggles!

EPILOGUE

AND THEN THERE WAS ONE....

Jorge Posada was two years into retirement, now an urbane, graying, sophisticated elder statesman free to be a Yankee Stadium presence at Old Timers Day and various other team celebrations, his pinstriped uniform replaced by a meticulously tailored pin-striped suit.

True to his word, Mariano Rivera, who had originally planned to retire after the 2012 season but who moved his retirement up a year after missing most of '12 with a torn ACL and a torn meniscus in his right knee, had announced that the 2013 major league season, his 19th, would be his last. He held to that oath, setting off a magical mystery farewell tour in cities throughout the American League.

Almost as an afterthought, Andy Pettitte came to the realization in the final days of the 2013 season that he could no longer endure the stress, strain, and physical agony he would surely suffer getting his almost 42-year-old body ready for another season and he, too, announced his retirement—*and this time he meant it.*

They had broken up the old gang, the Core Four. We had seen the last of a special breed, Buck Showalter told *New York Post* columnist Joel Sherman as the 2013 season and the careers of two members of the Core were winding down.

Showalter was manager of the Yankees in 1995 when Mariano Rivera, Andy Pettitte, Jorge Posada, and Derek Jeter showed up in the Bronx to be fitted for pinstripes. Now it was time to begin saying goodbye, and time for nostalgic reflection.

"You won't see anything like this happen again," Showalter said, meaning four players playing together with one team for so long and with such great success.

"There are too many variables for that to ever happen again. What you have to remember is the makeup of those guys. The common thread was their agenda. They didn't branch off. They didn't want to disappoint each other. They were guys who never wanted to let their teammates down.

"You know how hard it is to make as many good decisions on and off the field that those guys made for as long as they made them while playing in New York? They all had grips on reality at a young age in New York City. We just won't see that again."

They came, they stayed, they played, and now it was time to say goodbye. Only Derek Jeter was left. He was Paul without John, George, and Ringo; Jerry without George, Elaine, and Kramer. He was Theodore Roosevelt alone on Mount Rushmore.

For Rivera, the season-long festivities and the gift-giving began on April 7 in Detroit, when the Tigers honored him by bidding him *adieu* in a pregame ceremony at which they presented him with a plaque containing photos of Rivera pitching and bottles of dirt from the pitcher's mound of both the old (Tiger Stadium) and new (Comerica Park) Tigers' homes where Rivera had pitched.

Perhaps it was Rivera himself who had inadvertently planted the seed that would become his farewell tour when he asked Yankees officials for their help in arranging in each opponents' ballpark he visited in his final season a series of informal talks with selected small groups of invited guests, not team or city dignitaries, but average people, faithful fans, longtime team and stadium employees, old people and children, and the handicapped. He would hold these fan fests and in turn be feted in 16 cities in addition to New York.

In Cleveland, home of the Rock 'n' Roll Hall of Fame, he was presented with a gold record of the song "Enter Sandman" by the heavy metal group Metallica. Since 1999, the song had accompanied Rivera's entrance into a game at Yankee Stadium. (While it has been suggested that the song was selected for Rivera because according to legend the Sandman puts children to sleep, and Rivera's cutter puts batters to sleep, the connection with the name of the song is merely coincidental; "Enter Sandman" was chosen to accompany Rivera's entrance because of its rhythm and its intensity.)

And the gifts, some elaborate, some imaginative, just kept on coming. In Minnesota, Rivera received a rocking chair constructed with broken bats (a Rivera trademark and the brainchild of Twins' manager Ron Gardenhire). In Los Angeles, the Dodgers, noting that Rivera's father was a fisherman in his native Panama, presented him with a custom fishing rod. In Boston, the Red Sox gave him the bullpen pitching rubber and the placard No. 42 used to identify Mariano on the ancient manually operated Fenway Park scoreboard. In most cities he was presented with a generous check for the Mariano Rivera Foundation.

A highlight for Mariano in his final season would come on July 16, during the All-Star Game in Citi Field, home of the neighboring New York Mets. Rivera had been named to his 13th—and last—All-Star team. Before the game, several veteran American League All-Stars gave a dressing-room pep talk to their AL teammates. Rivera was among those that spoke.

"His speech was just about appreciation, how being a part of this game has meant so much" said Texas Rangers' closer Joe Nathan, Rivera's teammate for a day. "It was very respectful, very classy. He could have talked about peanut butter and jelly and we would have all been like, 'Yeah, that's pretty cool.' It was sweet."

It was hoped (expected?) that Rivera would be on the mound in the ninth inning to save the game for the American League as he had done four times before.

"I wanted to hear 'Enter Sandman' in the ninth," said Joe Nathan.

But Detroit Tigers manager Jim Leyland, managing the American League, had other ideas. He did not want to take any chances. He wanted to be certain Rivera got into the game so that he could receive an appropriate farewell. The AL scored a run in the top of the eighth inning to take a 3–0 lead, but Leyland feared that if the NL scored four runs in the bottom of the eighth, there would be no save situation in the ninth inning and no Mo. So as the National League prepared to bat in the bottom of the eighth, the strains of "Enter Sandman" could be heard throughout the stadium as Mo Rivera trotted in from the bullpen and into an eerie situation.

The crowd was on its feet giving him a warm and sustained reception. Rivera tipped his cap and then realized there were no American League teammates manning their positions behind him and no National League batters getting ready to step up to the plate. Players from both teams were on their feet in front of their respective dugouts applauding along with the fans. Both bullpens emptied and pitchers joined in the applause from the warning track. Rivera was taken aback.

"I wanted to come in and do my job," Rivera said. "When I got to the mound, I saw each team out of the dugout, cheering and applauding. It was amazing. It felt so weird. Basically, I was there alone with my catcher. I didn't know how to act. At that moment I didn't know what to do. Keep throwing the ball, I guess. It was so weird, but at the same time I appreciate what they did for me."

Rivera retired the National League in order in the eighth.

"It would have been better in the ninth, but we got him in the game, we got him his moment," said Nathan. "He was enjoying the moment, getting a chance to kind of reflect and look around and that was pretty cool."

The American League took its 3–0 lead into the bottom of the ninth as Leyland called on Nathan to save the game.

"My heart has never beat so fast," Nathan said. "I didn't know I was getting the ninth until the ninth."

He struck out Matt Carpenter and Andrew McCutchen, gave up a double to Paul Goldschmidt, and then nailed down the victory by getting Pedro Alvarez on a pop fly to second base.

Nathan has saved 341 major league games and he has the last ball from each of them. He had never before saved an All-Star game and this was a baseball he would cherish. But he knew the ball didn't belong to him. He gave it to Rivera.

"No brainer," Nathan said. "I wanted it, but I wanted to give it to him more. Outstanding. To be able to hand the ball over to him was pretty cool. It's no secret how much I look up to him and to be able to do that for him was awesome."

To Rivera, the whole night was "Amazing. I have no words. It was a wonderful night."

There would be many more wonderful nights, and days, for this man who had earned universal respect, admiration, and affection from teammates and opponents alike for his artistry on the field and his comportment off of it.

No night—or day—would be as wonderful as Sunday, September 22, "Mariano Rivera Day" at Yankee Stadium. A crowd of 49,197 came to pay homage to the Yankees' peerless closer, as did several of his former teammates, a former trainer, manager, and general manager.

Rachel and Sharon Robinson, the wife and daughter of the late Jackie Robinson, were there to witness Rivera's Yankees uniform No. 42 be permanently retired. (When Major League Baseball ordered all teams to retire uniform No. 42, those already wearing the number were grandfathered in to continue wearing No. 42 until they retired; Rivera was the last to do so.)

The Yankees presented Rivera with a rocking chair made of baseball bats, a framed replica of his retired number, a Waterford

Crystal replica of his 2013 glove, and a $100,000 check for his foundation.

And to close out the 50-minute celebration, the guest of honor stepped to the microphone to address the multitude.

Directing his remarks to the fans, he said, "It has been a great run, guys. You guys have been amazing. You always have been here for me and for the organization. I will never forget that. You guys will have part of my heart here in New York."

Four days later, the Yankees met the Tampa Bay Rays in their final home game of the season and the final game at Yankee Stadium in Mariano Rivera's career. When the Rays scored two runs in the top of the eighth to take a 4–0 lead and had runners on first and second with one out, manager Joe Girardi signaled to the bullpen and trotting into the game for the last time at Yankee Stadium came Mariano Rivera, who extinguished the rally without further scoring—no surprise—and returned to the mound for the ninth, the final inning of his career at Yankee Stadium.

Rivera retired the first two batters and was preparing to face his third batter when he was startled to see Derek Jeter and Andy Pettitte, two of his Core Fore compatriots, headed his way. It was a considerate gesture carefully planned by manager Joe Girardi, who wanted to give Mariano one final raucous ovation from a capacity Yankee Stadium crowd.

Girardi had to be aware of the historic nature of removing Rivera from the last game he would ever pitch in Yankee Stadium and he could have arranged to be the one to make that change. His decision to send Jeter and Pettitte to the mound to remove Rivera was not only theatric, it was inspired and selfless. Soon, Rivera could be seen embracing Pettitte tightly as the tears flowed from the eyes of both men, and from the eyes of thousands of others in the huge ballpark.

There were three games still on the Yankees schedule, all in Houston. Girardi said he was leaving it "up to Mo to pitch or not pitch; it's his call."

Rivera thought about it, decided it best to let the last pitch of his career come not in Houston, but in Yankee Stadium, the Bronx, New York, and pronounced himself all in.

"I've had enough," he said.

In truth, he had done more than enough.

In his final season, at age 43, he had a record of 6–2, 44 saves in 50 save opportunities, an earned run average of 2.11, 54 strikeouts and 17 walks in 64 innings and continued throughout the season to raise the question: "Why is this man retiring?"

Through it all, Rivera stuck to his guns. He was retiring to spend time with his family, to devote more time to his Foundation.

He had, indeed, had enough, unless you think 82 wins, 652 saves, a 2.21 earned run average, 1,173 strikeouts, and 286 walks in 1,283⅔ innings, are not enough for one career.

As the days dwindled down in the 2013 baseball season, Andy Pettitte found himself with a dilemma. He had known since spring training that the 2013 season would be his last, but he planned on waiting until the end of the season to make an announcement that would stamp his retirement as official. He realized, however, that by doing so, it might seem to some that he was raining on Rivera's parade or, in the least, hitching himself to Mariano's wagon. Neither was the truth, but he felt the need to make that clear to the one person that mattered, so four days before the big celebration, with the Yankees in Toronto, Pettitte invited Rivera to lunch.

"Mo was one of the guys that has known for a while that I was done and I was retiring," Pettitte said. "He all along has told me, 'You've got to announce it. You need to say something.' That's just not how I wanted to do it. I had planned on just announcing it at the end of the season."

But the thought that he might be intruding on Rivera's celebration or encroaching on Mo's spotlight haunted Pettitte and he unburdened himself by revealing his dilemma to Rivera over lunch in Toronto. Typically, Mariano put his friend at ease.

"He was so supportive," Pettitte recalled. "He told me I had to announce it and that I should. He said he thought it would make [Mariano Rivera Day] even better. To hear him say that, and to feel that way about it, I feel like we're connected."

Mariano Rivera Day at Yankee Stadium on September 22 became something of a dual celebration, but truly it was mostly Mariano's day, and Pettitte's involvement detracted from Rivera not one bit.

As fortune would have it, Pettitte started the game for the Yankees against the San Francisco Giants.

"I think he did the right thing, announcing his retirement and pitching in front of his fans," said a magnanimous Rivera. "That's the right way to do it."

Pettitte not only pitched, he excelled in a valiant effort to hold off the inevitable; the Yankees were sinking fast into an abyss of uncommon failure, inching toward elimination from contention for a postseason spot as an American League wild-card entrant. Pettitte did what he could to delay the inevitable, holding the Giants hitless through five and a third innings and to two hits through seven innings. "At this point, at this stage [at age 41, he was the oldest starting pitcher in the major leagues], I didn't think my body would allow me to pitch nine innings," he would say after the game. He left with the score tied 1–1 after giving up a leadoff double to Pablo Sandoval in the eighth and was tagged with the 2–1 loss when Sandoval scored.

Even in defeat, manager Joe Girardi heaped praise on his veteran warrior.

"One of the fiercest competitors that I've ever been around," said Girardi. "A man who got as much out of his talent as you could humanly possibly get. And that's the ultimate compliment for an athlete; a tremendous teammate!"

The Yankees were officially eliminated from pennant contention three days later (only the second time in the 19-year career of

Mariano Rivera that the Yankees did not advance to the postseason), but Pettitte was not done yet. The season would conclude for the Yankees with three games in Houston, and Pettitte would pitch the second game of the series, on a Saturday night, in a ballpark 20 miles from his hometown of Deer Park, Texas.

Pettitte breezed through three scoreless innings, then gave up a run in the fourth on a single and two infield outs. But the Yankees scored two in the sixth to give him a 2–1 lead and Pettitte protected the lead through a hitless sixth and seventh innings while facing only seven batters.

He had completed seven innings, and he was entering unfamiliar territory. He hadn't pitched a complete game since 2006, when he was with the Astros, and hadn't pitched one for the Yankees in 10 years, but he was fueled by adrenaline, by emotion, and by the positive energy from more than 50 friends and family in attendance, including his mom and dad, his wife, and his four children.

He retired the Astros in order in the eighth, two by strikeouts.

In the ninth, he got the first two batters on fly balls to right field, yielded a single to left and then, with his 116th pitch, got J.D. Martinez to hit a ground ball to third baseman Eduardo Nunez, who fired across the diamond to Lyle Overbay and the game was over. So, too, was Andy Pettitte's magnificent career.

He had evened his record for the season at 11–11, ending his career never having had a losing record in 18 major league seasons.

He finished his career with 256 victories, 42nd all-time, and with 2,448 strikeouts, 36th all-time. As a Yankee, he won 219 games, third all-time behind Hall of Famers Whitey Ford and Red Ruffing, and struck out 2,020 batters, the most for a Yankees pitcher.

Now Andy Pettitte could go into retirement in peace.

For two decades, Derek Jeter lived a charmed life, first-round pick by the New York Yankees in the 1992 major league amateur draft, American League Rookie of the Year in 1996, 13-time All-Star, possessor of five World Series rings, certain electee to the

Baseball Hall of Fame as soon as he becomes eligible, idol of millions, wealthy beyond his wildest dreams, escort to a bevy of the world's most beautiful women, intimate of some of the most famous, most powerful, most envied, and most influential people in the world.

And then it was 2013.

Derek Jeter, who had averaged 151 games a season for the previous 17 years, played in 17 games; who had accumulated 2,992 career hits, had only 12; who had hit 255 major league home runs, hit one; who had averaged 73 RBI a season, drove in seven; who had scored 1,863 runs, scored eight; who had compiled a career batting average of .313, batted .190.

For someone who never admitted he was hurting, who brushed off injuries and took pride in playing every day, even when he was hurt, who hated sitting and watching, hated not competing, not contributing, the season was "a nightmare."

On September 11, with the Yankees in third place in the American League East, 10½ games out of first but still not mathematically eliminated from making the playoffs, Jeter had no choice but to give in to the inevitable. He was going on the disabled list for the fourth time. His season was over. In his absence, the Yankees would use seven shortstops, from Reid Brignac to Brendan Ryan.

"It's very disappointing not to be able to play, especially this time of year," he said. "This is when I want to play the most. Unfortunately, that's not the case. The entire year has been pretty much a nightmare for me physically, so I guess it's fitting that it ends like this."

The nightmare actually began the previous year, October 13, 2012, in Yankee Stadium, when he fractured his left ankle while fielding a ground ball in the 12th inning of the first game of the American League Championship Series against Detroit and was writhing in pain in the dirt around second base. One week later he underwent surgery on the ankle and vowed to be ready for the following season opener. He went to work conscientiously to achieve that goal.

But two weeks before the start of the season, he was scratched from starting an exhibition game in Clearwater, Florida, because of stiffness in his left ankle. On April 18, it was discovered he had a new small fracture of the surgically repaired left ankle and was put on the disabled list. He would make his first start of the season on July 11 against the Kansas City Royals at Yankee Stadium in the Yankees' 92nd game of the season.

Batting second as the designated hitter, Jeter would get an infield single on a weak ground ball to third base in his first at-bat. Later he would ground out weakly to second base, shortstop, and third base, but strained his right quad running the bases and was placed on the disabled list a second time.

He returned to the lineup on July 28 and, in typical dramatic fashion, Jeter hit a home run in his first at-bat against Tampa Bay Rays young lefthander Matt Moore.

"He's a movie," said Joe Girardi.

Jeter later singled and grounded out twice in a 6–5 Yankees victory. He would play four games on his comeback before being put back on the disabled list with a strained right calf.

This time, he would miss almost a month, returning to the lineup on August 11 in Toronto. On September 7, he singled in the sixth inning against the Red Sox, the 3,316th hit of his career, moving him past Eddie Collins for 10th (and only three behind Paul Molitor for ninth, 103 behind Carl Yastrzemski for eighth, and 104 behind Honus Wagner for seventh) on the all-time list. But Joe Girardi didn't like the way Jeter ran to first and removed him from the game.

"You feel horrible for him," said Andy Pettitte. "You know how bad he wants to be out there. For him to come out of a game, he was hurt, so it wasn't surprising. I hate it. I hate it for him!"

Four days later, Jeter was placed on the disabled list for the fourth time and acknowledged in talks with the local media that his season was over.

What next?

"I'll grab some pom-poms and root for my teammates," Jeter said. "I've had pom-poms for a lot of this season already. You just try to help out as much as you can, in any way that you can. Root for your teammates. My teammates have rooted for me enough over the years. Now it's my turn."

Had he reached the end of an illustrious career?

"There's a lot of end talk here, man," he said, bristling slightly at the innuendos. "Do you guys want this to be the end for me? It seems that's what everyone is asking. Have I thought about it? No. I don't think about the end of anything. I've tried to come back this year as quickly as possible every time I came back and looking back maybe that wasn't the best thing to do. But my job now is to get ready for next year and I'll do that."

As the season played itself out with Jeter in the unaccustomed role of cheerleader, the major question was about 2014.

There was a $9.5 million option (Jeter's) that would bring him back for 2014, but in what role?

Jeter faced an uncertain future. Would he return? Would he be able to get back to his physical peak? Would he be able to play shortstop? Would he have to swallow his enormous pride, move over to make room for a younger player and switch to another position?

With six months to rehabilitate his injuries before the start of spring training, and all of spring training to hone his skills, Jeter was optimistic about the future.

"There is no doubt in my mind that I will be back to where I was," he said. "I'm not thinking about getting hurt again. It sounds kind of funny saying it now considering how many times I've been hurt, but I truly believe with a full off-season of working out and getting my strength back that I'll get back to doing what I've always done."

"There are no guarantees," said Joe Girardi, "but I will never doubt Derek because of who he is. If he believes he can get back, I believe him. That's the bottom line."

"I have not watched his last game," said Yankees' general manager Brian Cashman. "Nobody has."

Still, the hard, cold facts, the undeniable truth, is in Jeter's age. He will be 40 years old before the 2014 season is half over and we are reminded that there have been only three shortstops that played at least 100 games at the age of 40 or older and they hardly played up to their previous productivity.

But none of the three was named Derek Sanderson Jeter.